POWER STEPS

RELEASING THE FORCE WITHIN

LICE THOMAS & PERCY THOMAS

Outskirts Press, Inc.
http://www.outskirtspress.com

ISBN: 978-1-4787-0900-8

Outskirts Press and the "OP" logo are trademarks belonging to Outskirts Press, Inc.

PRINTED IN THE UNITED STATES OF AMERICA

TABLE OF CONTENTS

ACKNOWLEDGMENTS

We would like to express our gratitude to the many people who supported us through the writing of this book. Specifically, we would like to thank our dear friend, Claudette Guilford, for providing access to her home in the mountains of West Virginia to write this book. It provided a peaceful sanctuary.

We would also like to express our sincere thanks to our son Dr. Joseph E. Hines, who encouraged us to write the book, read drafts, and provided key insights.

Lastly, but not least, we would like to thank all of the individuals who have over the years used and helped us to improve these principles.

FOREWORD

Dr.'s Percy and Alice Thomas have done it again, <u>Power Steps: Releasing the Force Within</u> has taken the art of learning how to achieve success to another level!! The authors are amazingly successful, yet humble individuals who I am thankful are willing to share with the world how they have achieved their success.

They have accomplished the highest level of educational achievement, the highest levels of promotion in their federal government careers, and the highest levels of status and prominence in their academic professions, and private sector organizations. They are business owners, authors, property owners, and believers in a higher power. It is one thing to have authors who are sharing what they believe success to be, it's entirely another to have those who have experienced success share with you how they did it.

Thirteen years ago, I was introduced to Percy's first

book, <u>Power Steps: 10 Principles of Success</u>, in manuscript form and it literally changed my life. I was at a crossroads because I was retiring from the military and contemplating my next steps. Then, I read Power Steps and knew just what I needed to do. It was what I had been doing my entire life. I intuitively knew what it took to be successful, but I did not know that I knew. For those of you who have experienced <u>Power Steps: 10 Principles of Success</u> you understand what I'm speaking of. The book was like "yeah" that's what I did when I was successful at accomplishing that goal or achieving that dream. For others, the principles provide the essential elements of the formula for success that you were missing.

We who have been on the Power Steps journey have now been able to take intuitive steps and make them intentional. We also had a secret weapon because we were taught not only the 10 Principles, but we were also taught the incredible part the *"mind"* plays in applying each principle to our lives. This was another intuitive part of becoming successful that many of us knew but that others didn't.

<u>Power Steps: Releasing the Force Within</u> makes the intuitive intentional. It is like <u>Power Steps: 10 Principles of Success</u> on steroids or an all-natural herbal supplement. Steroids have a bad name, but doctors use them to expedite the healing process in a safe and healthy

manner, and herbal supplements are intended for the same purpose. When used correctly these supplements stimulate growth and speed up the natural restorative processes of the mind and body.

Power Steps: Releasing the Force Within speeds up the success process by injecting the intuitive process of how the **"mind"** impacts our success with the inclusion of intentional practices that anyone can incorporate into their lives. The *"mind"* is the missing piece to the puzzle, the secret that will unlock the door to your ultimate success. Power Steps: 10 Principles of Success helped many of us achieve great levels of success. Power Steps: Releasing the Force Within will help many more achieve even greater levels faster. It's **Power Steps on Steroids!**

Let your next step be a Power Step, thank you Percy and Alice for once again impacting lives and changing the world one Power Step at a time.

Love you,

"Dr. J"

Joseph E. Hines, Ph.D.
President/CEO
Success Business Inc. (SBI)

PREFACE

This book is predicated on 10 principles presented in my first book _Power Steps: 10 Principles of Success_ (Power Steps). In Power Steps, I presented the 10 Principles as a practical guide for those seeking success in their lives. I made every effort to make these time-tested principles clear and actionable. Based on feedback about the book from many people who attended our seminars, workshops, and the Power Steps Fireside Chats, held in our home, I saw evidence of having achieved that goal.

My wife Alice Thomas, who is the co-author of this book, provided me with additional feedback from her observations of people's reactions at the Fireside Chats. Her take was that while people enjoyed reading the book and discussing the principles, they wanted more information about how to apply and use the principles daily. Many of them had learned all 10 principles and could discuss them with others, but when asked what made the principles work for them, they could not answer the question. Take the principle of belief, they knew what it meant and that it could produce what they believed to be true. What they did not know is how a strongly held belief has the power to influence positive or negative behavior. What was missing is how beliefs connect to the mind to affect behavior. Based on having to explain this concept at our Fireside Chats and seminars, Alice was convinced that I should write a new book connecting the 10 Principles to the Mind.

One day while driving, I heard on the radio that the *"Mind is a terrible thing to waste."* It's a well-known phrase and I've heard it many times, but this time I immediately reflected on what Alice said about writing another book that focused on the connection of the principles to the mind. The thought of writing another book was not something I wanted to do, or was it? From the time Alice mentioned another book, I began to think about it. After a while, every day I saw events and heard about situations that stimulated my thinking about the need for a revision and second edition of Power Steps. When I discussed my ideas with Alice, she gave me more ideas. The difference is that she is a pragmatist, so after the third time of discussing the new book, she asked me when I was going to start writing. I told her I would only write another book on Power Steps if she consented to be the co-author. She consented, and we began developing a shared vision. I could spend the next few pages telling you about what a blessing it is to be equally yoked. Instead, we just thank God for each other's receptivity, creativity, and let's do it attitudes.

The mind is very powerful and once you feed it ideas it will take over and fill in the blanks. For several weeks we bounced ideas around about how we would anchor the concept of the mind in the new book. Each time by simply talking about the subject we realized that we became excited and energized. It was as though the very core of our being was catching on fire. Some of the concepts we discussed are contained in the list below, but the one that energized us the most was the discussion of the *force within you*.

1. Mind Power
2. Achieve what you Dream About
3. Keys to Success Inside Your Head
4. Be What You Think About
5. **The Force Within**
6. Mindset the Power of Change
7. The Mind and Your future
8. Think your Way to Success
9. Success is In Your Thoughts
10. Be What the Mind Sees

After agreeing on the direction, the book would take, we realized how easy it was to make the connection between the new book and <u>Power Steps: 10 Principles</u>

of Success because the concepts regarding the **"mind"** have always been the 800lb. elephant in the room. Over the years of teaching and using the principles, we had mastered and internalized the concepts and linkages between the Mind and the 10 Principles without fully realizing that they were missing from the first book.

At our seminars, we talked about the force within all of us and passionately described how the 10 Principles were tools that when used systematically showed us how to release and sustain our desired dreams and goals. Each time we talked about the principles, we suddenly felt like Obi-Wan Kenobi, a Jedi, with the power to release the force from within. In fact, I can remember Alice, jokingly, ending a couple of the seminars with the statement, *"Now go forth and release the force within you."*

The 10 Principles and their connection to the force within each human being to have, be, and do what they want in life is the main focus of this book. The principles and steps in this book can be used to open your mind to a world of possibilities and success. By learning the principles and practicing the steps presented you can place yourself in the driver's seat toward a successful career, a thriving business, a super marriage, and many loving relationships.

Not only can you have what you want. You can have

what you want when you want it, and anytime you decide to go after it. Getting what you want is not magic. Rather, it is the deliberate application of Power Steps and the knowledge of how to use the *force within you* that is covered in this book.

We know the principles work when followed consistently, for they have worked for us in every aspect of our lives, and they will work for you. The secret to the success you want in life lies in your learning and applying these principles to *release the force within you* to have what you desire, be who you want to be, and do what you want to do in life. Since writing Power Steps: 10 Principles of Success, we have witnessed the principles at work for many people who have studied them and used them as a tool to achieve success.

In this book, we build on the 10 principles presented in the first book by showing how the power of the Mind links to Vision and Beliefs and discussing how the other principles support and bring balance to the total model. Also, we have strengthened the notion that the Power Step principles convert the words in the model to mental programs that become the software of your mind. They compel you to achieve success once the words are understood and accepted in the Subconscious Mind. Once you begin to apply these principles in your daily life, you will begin to experience success on whatever course you embark. With the mastery of these principles, you become the master of your own destiny. This book opens the treasure chest of life which rest in ***releasing the force within you*** to be truly the super person each of us was born to be.

This book is intended to jump start you on the path to realizing your hopes and dreams, now. To get immediate results out of this book, you must read it and teach its contents to another person or group. Why teach it to someone else? Because we teach best what we need to know ourselves.

Percy W. Thomas, Sc.D.
Laytonsville, Maryland
January, 2018

INTRODUCTION

*"The value of one's worth to others is in his actions.
The value of one's worth to himself is in his thoughts."*
—Percy W. Thomas

Why was Power Steps Written?

When Power Steps was first conceived and presented in 1987, it was a sixty-minute PowerPoint presentation. It was primarily a motivation talk directed at college students, and employees working in federal, state and local governments. As more people were exposed to Power Steps, we began to get requests to make presentations at public and private sector national conferences. Many non-profit mental health organizations across the Country requested presentations for their staffs as a method to recharge their batteries and to continue having success in their difficult jobs.

The demand for Power Steps continued to increase to the point that by the end of 1987, we decided to start Success Behavior Institute (SBI). Teachers at the elementary, middle, and high school levels wanted Power Steps taught to their students. The Maryland State College National Alumni Association included Power Steps in its Alumni Career Opportunities Enhancement (ACOE) program, and for several years at the Blacks in Government (BIG) National Conferences, in a room set for hundreds, there was standing room only. In 2005, we reinstituted the concept of the Franklin Delano Roosevelt Fireside Chats[1] in our home to provide an opportunity for people to focus on the principles in an informal and supportive forum. Many people who attended the Fireside Chats have gone on to be entrepreneurs, landlords, authors of books, and creators of organizations. In 2015, we were proud to say that *Power Steps* had reached the ears of thousands of individuals seeking to ignite a spark in their lives and the lives of others to achieve success.

It is safe to say that Lillian Taylor Thomas, (Percy's Mother) and Evelyn Thomas Labode (Percy's Sister) both deceased, would be proud to know that the sayings Lillian repeated over and over to her two children resulted in both of them achieving success in their professional and personal lives. We are also sure that she

---

[1]   Fireside chats is the term used to describe a series of 28 evening radio addresses given by U.S. President Franklin D. Roosevelt between 1933 and 1944.

would be proud to know that the sayings she reared her children and lived her life by have helped so many people, and she would be doubly proud that her sayings are the basis for another book, _Power Steps: Releasing the Force Within_.

Below are some of the sayings of this remarkable lady whose ancestral origins began in Africa, survived slavery, endured Jim Crow and lived a fruitful life. I am sure that many of you have heard similar ones in your homes and we are proud to give them a legacy in memory of Lillian in this book.

Lillian Thomas' Sayings	
• Learn something new everyday	• What goes around comes around
• When you believe you will receive.	• Reach for the stars
• Dream Big	• There is nothing you cannot have or be
• The early bird catches the worm.	• Anything worth doing is worth doing well
• There is no free ride.	• To accomplish anything you must do the work

Power Steps Journey

Over the last 30 years _Power Steps_ has taken us on a fantastic journey. We have traveled to more than forty states teaching the *Power Steps* principles. We lived in the United Arab Emirates and shared the principles with employees and students of the Higher Colleges of Technology. Power Steps has allowed us to interact with children of all ages, educators, business executives, and heads of non-profit organizations to bring a simple message of *"if you believe it you can achieve it."*

We also consider the success of our friends and children, who have bought into the principles and used them to catapult themselves to successful careers and business ventures. As evidence of the effect *Power Steps* can have when fully accepted and applied, our son, Dr. Joseph Hines, who embraced the principles before he retired from the Navy, has used Power Steps to launch a spin-off of Success Behavior Institute. His company, Success Business Inc. is a successful organizational development consulting company and he has written a book a <u>Personal Walk</u>, which incorporates the *Power Steps'* principles.

As the audiences exposed to *Power Steps* grew, Joseph was instrumental in assisting us with incorporating Success Behavior Institute, branding the company as *SBI*, conducting the seminars, Fireside Chats, and developing a training of trainer's series. Memorable for us is the first group of five individuals that went through the training of trainer's program and are now successful professionals. Chad Newkirk, who entered the federal government at the journeyman level and quickly became a senior administrator. In his spare time Chad is a successful Real Estate Investor; Michael Lloyd gained the confidence to start a security business and pursue a Ph.D.; Melissa Robertson another successful federal executive and Real Estate investor; George Clark, also a federal employee, who developed the skills to be promoted to a middle manager, and Rev. Jacob Lee, who while serving as a Chaplin in the military saw how Power Steps served as a motivation for his spiritual beliefs.

This journey with *Power Steps* has personally allowed our friends and us to grow as people and reinforce that there is a great power in the universe that extends beyond the boundaries of human control. That power is the Creator, who extends that power to us in the form of a life force. We are collectively more cognizant of the fact that if people learn about the power that is within them, they can be more proactive in setting and achieving their goals.

Alice and I have thought about this statement, which is written in the first *Power Steps* book, *"The Value of one's worth to others is in his actions, and the value of one's worth to himself is in his thoughts."* Reflecting on the statement and realizing that it relates to how successful people propel themselves to become successful, we decided to use the statement as the springboard for this book.

We have come to believe strongly in the notion that one's thoughts hold the key to how a person sees him or herself. Further we believe that one's actions are produced by his or her thoughts and therefore correlate strongly with how others view their worth.

We believe the value of one's worth or their value to others plays an important part in the goals they establish for themselves in their careers, avocations, relationship with others, and their purpose in life. Values are reflective of how some individuals think. Thus, the quality of and intensity of your thoughts are relevant to what you are capable of demonstrating to self and others. To make manifest what you value, think, and believe you must first understand how your mind works. Your mind holds the key to making possible what you think about and believe to be true.

We would not be writing this book if we did not first think about writing it and secondly believe that we could write it. Once we accepted the thought and believed strongly in its value to others and ourselves, it became a strong purpose. Once it became our purpose (our raison d'être), we were put on automatic pilot to start writing this book.

What does it mean to be put on automatic pilot? Your mind takes over and compels you to do something; in our case, writing the book. You begin to see, hear, and understand things that relate to your purpose. It is as if you suddenly have the capacity to block all distractions and focus with clarity on that which you are thinking about. Moreover, it is as though some force controls your waking and sleeping hours with deep concentration on achieving that which is reflected in the thoughts and beliefs you hold.

The overarching theme of <u>Power Steps: Releasing the Force Within</u> is all about achieving the success that human beings desire in their lives. Further, it is building on the 10 principles presented in the first book. <u>Merriam Webster</u> defines success as: 1) a degree or measure of succeeding; 2) a favorable desired outcome or 3) the attainment of wealth, favor, or eminence. <u>The Encarta World Dictionary</u> defines success as the following: "*1) achievement of a desired aim, the achievement of something planned or attempted; 2) attainment of fame, wealth, or power: impressive achievement, especially the attainment of fame, wealth, or power; 3) something that turns out well or something that turns out as planned or intended; 4) somebody who has significant achievements or somebody who has a record of achievement, especially in gaining wealth, fame, or power.*"

Power Steps: Releasing the Force Within goes beyond just presenting the principles of success to explaining how to use the principles in tandem with your **mind** to invent and reinvent yourself to fulfill and change your purpose in life. We hope that by reading this book you will come to understand that you possess a **force within you** that has the capacity to enable you to change and achieve. This force knows no boundaries or limitations and everything is possible. Thus, the only limitations other than those placed on us by physical constraints are self imposed.

By understanding the force within you, you will be better able to apply the 10 principles, to rid yourself of self imposed limitations, and to achieve true success in the goals you set for yourself.

Power Steps Lexicon

Presented in the table below are words that we believe are important for you to learn and incorporate into your mindset as triggers in applying the principles in this book.

Power Steps Lexicon	
Concepts	Meaning
1. Psychological Energy	1. Beliefs, attitudes, values, and behavior
2. Physical Energy	2. General nutrition, diet, exercise, and rest
3. Social Intelligence	3. Intellect used to build rapport with and get along with others
4. Emotional Energy	4. Emotional self-control of anger, stress, and unwanted behavior

5. Force Within	5. Your mind and how you choose to use it, as well as, the effort to get what you want; the power to become what you want to be; the power within to invent or reinvent yourself.
6. Power	6. The ability to do good and bad things as well as the power to take charge of your life and make the necessary changes to overcome any obstacles in your path.
7. Work	7. Getting things done and executing things with ease
8. Strength	8. Mental strength, physical strength, strength in building strong relationships
9. Light	9. Creating a vision and clearly seeing yourself achieving success
10. Theatricality	10. Acting your way into behaving successfully; using sense memory and emotional memory. The whole world is a stage and you are the main character in the play of life and success.
11. Mind	11. A complex mental construct in humans that initiates perceptions, feelings, and triggers rationalization, will and truth through the interrelationship of the conscious and unconscious.

12. Possibility	12. What you see or dream and your mind believes to be true without barriers or limitations.
13. Autonomic Nervous System	13. The part of the nervous system that controls all involuntary bodily functions not consciously performed; such as, breathing, the heartbeat, and digestive system process.

ONE

HOW THE MIND WORKS

"The eye sees only what the mind
is prepared to comprehend."
—Henri Bergson

When we think of the power of the mind, we think of the moral written in the book *Acres of Diamonds,* by Russell H. Blackwell. Blackwell tells a story about a man who was well off and became discontent after hearing how much more wealtheir he could be if he had diamonds. He was told that diamonds could be found **"where a river ran through white sand and between two mountains"** and that if he wanted them all he had to do was go out and find them. His mind was instantly filled with thoughts of acquiring diamonds to become rich. He sold his farm and went in search of diamonds because of the discontentment that built up in his mind regarding his lack of diamonds; ultimately, he became a poor man. Years later, destitute, distraught, and depressed he ended his life. The point of this story is that the mind is a powerful source in determining what you will or will not do in life.

The diamond seeker achieved his desired success. Now, perhaps you are beginning to question our sanity at this point, since the man lost all his worldly material possessions and ultimately his life. And, maybe you are thinking that because he did not find diamonds he was not successful. To the contrary, he was successful in fulfilling his desire to <u>search</u> for diamonds. It was his mind that enabled him to sell his worldly treasures and go in search of them. It was his mind that placed him on automatic pilot for moving out on what he believed to be true. As you question our sanity, let me make it clear that the mind is capable of producing success or failure. The caution for each of us is that the mind does not decide what we choose to do; rather, it helps us fulfill what we believe to be true. Your mind will work for you to achieve success in any endeavor based on the direction you give it (Murphy, 2009). To fully understand the mind and how it works in pursuing your goals, you must learn its functions.

What is the Mind?

The Mind is viewed by many as the intellect and

consciousness regulator of the brain and is responsible for our thoughts, emotions, perceptions, memories, and creative and cognitive processes (Maultsby, 1975). Most often we associate the mind with words such as conscious and unconscious. Many scholars view the mind as two parts: Conscious and Subconscious mind. In this book, we will examine the Mind in three parts and use the terms Conscious, Subconscious, and Creative Subconscious.

The Mind in Three Parts

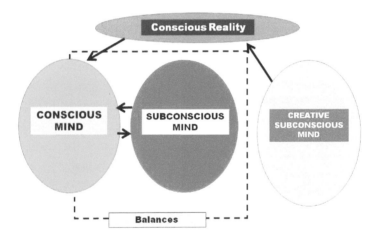

In 1987, we attended a workshop in Seattle, Washington titled, "Investment in Excellence," and Lou Tice, founder of the Pacific Institute, taught a module on the <u>Mind</u>. He introduced concepts about the Conscious, Subconscious, and Creative Subconscious that changed our lives. We learned that the power of the Subconscious Mind was the repository of truth, and that any thoughts sustained in the Subconscious Mind as truth would place your behavior on automatic pilot. Frequently, throughout the workshop he would say, "if you believe it you can achieve it." On the flight back to Washington, D.C., we vowed to start using the concepts in terms of how we functioned as consultants. Included in our Vision was how we would price our services. Prior to the workshop, when we examined our costs, despite current trends and the actual cost of our services, we told ourselves that we couldn't possibly state that amount as our fee. It was scary to think how much business we might lose with this new approach. We remember practicing how we would state our price and how giddy and thrilled we were when one day someone simply said, OK.

Once we started embracing the concepts of the Mind in our lives, we found ourselves connecting the dots to other theories. In 1990, Dr. Maxie Maultsby, Jr., a renowned psychiatrist, and the founder of Rational Behavior Therapy taught Percy in his Rational Behavior Therapy training program that the brain is the main organ of learning and self-control, and the mind is the totality of brain functions. Basically, the brain is the physical organ that makes it possible for the mind to initiate learning and self control. Tice and Maultby's contributions have become central to our belief that understanding the functions of the mind is essential to taking control of one's success.

When we first started presenting <u>Power Steps: 10 Principles of Success</u>, people who heard the presentations became excited and wanted to use them right away. Shortly, after they attempted to apply the Principles, however, we would receive phone calls, from many of them, saying that they were having difficulty using the Principles. We were in a quandary as to what to tell them because there were many other people who had heard the presentations and read the book who were applying the Principles and experiencing success in their lives. For instance, our son Joseph Hines read Power Steps on a flight back to Bahrain. When he got off the plane, he called us and said that the Principles were great, and he saw how he could use them to prepare for what he would do after retiring from the Navy. He was fired up and did not need any further explanations or support to make the Principles work for him. Perhaps, he and a few others were the exceptions because over time, we discovered that the vast majority of people that were exposed to the Principles needed to be taught how to apply the Principles to their lives.

After, a period of being in denial about the shortcomings of the book _Power Steps: 10 Principles of Success_, we decided to take an objective look at the feedback we got from participants who had read the book or attended a fireside chat and/or workshop. We went back to school on the subject of success by reading and re-reading the works of several scholars and other authors: Aristotle, Claude M. Bristol, Anton Chekhov, Albert Ellis, Erick Erikson, Victor Frankl, Sigmund Freud, Zayd Abdul-Karim, Maxie Maultsby, Norman Vincent Peale, Harold Sherman, Socrates, as well as the men who wrote the books of the Bible. What we learned from the great writers we studied is that in some fashion, they knew that the "mind" was the trigger for success.

In *Power Steps: 10 Principles of Success*, the importance of the Mind was <u>not</u> adequately addressed. What was needed is a basic understanding of how the principles work in tandem with the mind to produce success, by activating the *force within you* to achieve what your heart desires. This may sound to you like we are saying that the force within is a super natural power. If you have concluded that as our meaning, great! That is exactly what we are saying. So, let us say it clearly, the "**Force Within You**" is a supernatural power. All healthy human beings are born with this power; however, most people don't know how to use it.

Before we move forward on breaking down the mind, we think it worthwhile to set the environment in which the three functions (conscious, subconscious and creative subconscious) of the mind are activated. Tice and

Maultsby reference the mind as the triggers for what we think, feel, and do. It is within this context that we posit actions of the mind with its three distinct functions in connection with our Conscious Reality.

Conscious Reality

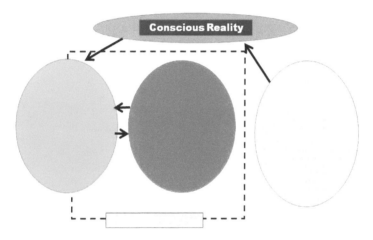

The Conscious Reality is the real world in which we live and function. It is the source of our daily human encounters with people, events and situations. Events such as weather, interacting with people, going to church, driving a car, listening to a teacher, eating a meal, hearing a concert, playing a game, and falling in love are all examples of being present in one's Conscious Reality. Our experiences in Conscious Reality are the source of our ideas, beliefs, and thoughts. Everything we encounter in Conscious Reality is transmitted via our brain (the physical organ) to our Conscious Mind (source of perceptions and awareness) and processed through our five senses of seeing, touching, hearing, tasting and smelling. From a success perspective, what we choose to focus on in Conscious Reality matters. If you choose negative experiences such as stealing, gambling, extortion, prostitution and spend an inordinate amount of time watching, demeaning, devaluing, and self-deprecating programs you run the risk of having a whole host of negative ideas and beliefs transmitted to your Conscious Mind.

Conscious Mind

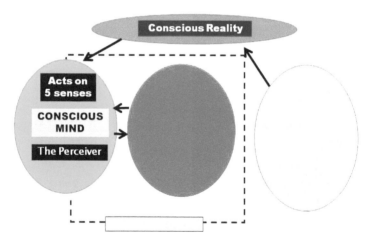

In our model of the Mind, the Conscious Mind acts as the perceiver of life events and situations that occur in one's daily environment. Using the five senses (seeing, hearing, smelling, tasting, and feeling), the Mind converts all ideas, beliefs, thoughts, and behaviors resulting from life experiences to messages that are sent to the Subconscious Mind. These messages convert to intuition and emotions in the Subconscious Mind that drives and sustains your convictions and behaviors. So, what you believe and become in life begins with the perceptions you allow to enter your Conscious Mind. Your Conscious Mind is the Guard of your Subconscious Mind to protect it from negative and false messages about yourself and your goals. Just as a Guard has the authority and responsibility to reject access to a military base, the Conscious Mind has the power to disallow negative and untrue messages from entering your Subconscious Mind. It is important to know that suggestions, ideas, beliefs, and thoughts cannot be imposed on the Subconscious Mind without the concurrence of the Conscious Mind. Thus, always be mindful of what you think and believe about what you see, hear, touch, smell, and taste because of its impact on the Subconscious Mind.

Today, we have so many examples of people allowing their Conscious Reality experiences to become accepted practices for their Conscious Mind. Harmful experiences with drugs, alcohol, sex, cigarettes, and criminal activities accepted by the Conscious Mind as pleasurable and rewarding often lead to addictive behaviors.

While we could cite example after example from historical events, and recent newspaper articles, we write about this from our personal experience with one of our children, who was introduced to the enterprise of illegal drugs. He grew up in a middle-class home undergirded with Christian values and practices. It seemed that our belief that education should be a part of one's foundation was resonating with him. He was smart and as a kid had always exhibited an entrepreneurial and nurturing spirit. In College, he figured out a way to make biscuits in his dorm room, expanded to chicken and biscuits and became well-known for his morning and late night snacks. Having completed two years of college with average grades, we thought he was well on his way to following family tradition. Yet, when he turned 18, he was introduced to the profits associated with selling drugs and pimping women in the inner city and he chose a different path. Though, he never used drugs, he became addicted to the lifestyle that fast money afforded him. We wish we could tell you he turned his life around; in fact, he was murdered two weeks prior to his 25th birthday.

Writing about "*Power Steps*" and presenting the concepts to others has helped us to recognize how his personality and the allure of selling drugs and pimping women created for him success. He loved the environment of his Conscious Reality. His Conscious Mind believed that because he grew up in a family environment that was different from the people he associated with, he knew how to protect himself, and would not become contaminated. He believed that he could associate with and be around the evils of the illegal drug enterprise and still be safe. What he was unaware of is how his Conscious Reality was interacting with the Conscious Mind to redefine his values and truths that reside in the Subconscious Mind. He was no longer the same because what you think about and pass on to the Subconscious Mind becomes the truth that will guide your behavior and what you will become.

Subconscious Mind

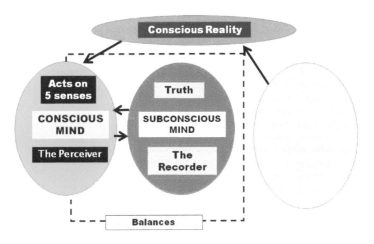

We believe that the Subconscious Mind controls all of our purpose-driven behaviors. To understand fully the workings of the Subconscious Mind *[the force within you]* and its power, we must know how it relates to our beliefs, attitudes and values. Whatever beliefs, attitudes, and values we accept as truths on the subconscious level is recorded and predisposes us to certain behaviors. **Beliefs** are mental constructs that cause humans to take action without the occurrence of an event or stimuli. Holding a strongly held belief about an event or situation negatively or positively, will produce behavior associated with the nature of the belief.

An **attitude** is a constellation of beliefs that aggregate to predispose us to take action once an event occurs or a situation presents itself. Our behavior will always be consistent with the nature of our attitude. For example, if a person believes his room has a snake in it and he holds the following beliefs about snakes, i.e., "they are dangerous," "if it bites me I will die," "they attack people without cause," or "it will paralyze me," they will behave in accordance with their beliefs. Consequently, given their attitude about snakes, you would not be surprised to see them run from the mere appearance of a snake.

Our **values** are represented by our deepest held beliefs. Our values are based on beliefs that are central to who we are, and if eliminated, would have to be replaced with values of equal value and importance.

Our beliefs, attitudes, and values sustained in our Subconscious are responsible for all behaviors not resulting from our autonomic nervous system. All behaviors that result from our thinking stems from our Subconscious Mind. Thus, the life we choose and our success in it is dependent on our thinking and ultimately the *force within you*.

Many philosophers, psychologist, and psychiatrist believe that whatever your Conscious Mind perceives as true, your Subconscious Mind accepts without scrutiny and will make happen. In our Model of the Mind the Subconscious Mind is the recorder of the truth and it works in tandem with the Conscious Mind. It takes what the Conscious Mind conveys to it and acts upon it. This is why so many people believe in the concept set forth by James Allen in a little book published in 1902 titled <u>As a Man Thinketh</u>. The title of the book suggests that what you think will become true for you in life. Allen was building on the biblical verse in Proverbs Chapter 23: 7. *"For as he thinketh in his heart, so is he: Eat and drink, saith he to thee; but his heart is not with thee."* During biblical times when the writers wrote of the heart they were referring to the mind because in those days there was no word for mind. The part of the mind Allen is referring to is the Subconscious Mind. The following passage from Allen's book sums up the power of the mind in general and in specific the power of the Subconscious Mind:

"The soul attracts that which it secretly harbors, that which it loves, and also that which it fears. It reaches the height of its cherished aspirations. It falls to the level of its unchastened desires—and circumstances are the means by which the soul receives its own."

We cannot read Allen's words without thinking about our son. *"The soul attracts that which it secretly harbors,…….."* Each of us has the power to choose happiness or sadness, and we have the power to define what success looks like in our lives. We <u>can</u> select a life pursuit that brings joy and contentment <u>or</u> one that fills our lives with unhappiness, displeasure, and discontent. The mechanism by which you accomplish either relates to the thoughts you hold as truth(s) in your Subconscious Mind. What we accomplish or do not accomplish in our lives, for the most part, has a direct correlation with what we believe and think that gets communicated as truth on the subconscious level of our mind. Such thoughts and beliefs predetermine our future and the success we reach. For many the notion that we are in charge of our progression in life and our success is frightening. This is due largely to our propensity as human beings to doubt ourselves and/ or fix blame on others for our failures and inadequacies. We like to believe that who we are and what we will become happens by magic, or some mystical being waves a wand and it all just happens without any thinking on our part.

At this point, some of you who have been traveling on a negative path are wondering if you can turn your life around. The good news is that the negative programming of your Subconscious Mind can be changed. Remember, if you change how you think you can change, because you can change your acceptance/interpretation of what you experience in your Conscious Reality.

For example, individuals who first experience the high from an injection of heroin say they get sick. They experience what some describe as a "good sick" feeling. If the Conscious Mind had perceived the first experience with heroine as a "bad sick" feeling, it would have communicated to the Subconscious Mind a bad sickness and the Subconscious Mind would accept it as true and reject any future behavior associated with heroin use. We surmise that this is why some individuals that have experimented with heroin and other hard drugs and decided it was not a good feeling have avoided all future use of illegal drugs. This attitude/belief allows the Conscious Mind to block the Subconscious Mind from receiving and recording the experience, and seeking knowledge on how you turn around negative predispositions for failure. That is the job of the Creative Subconscious Mind.

Creative Subconscious Mind

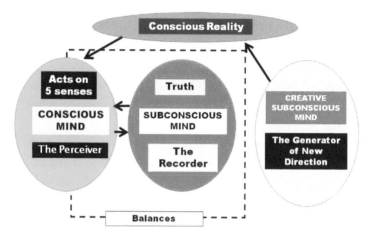

As we stated earlier, the concept of the Creative Subconscious Mind was introduced to us through the teachings of Lou Tice. What follows in this section is essentially an invisible collaboration and improvisation of his teachings regarding the function of the Creative Subconscious. In our Model of the Mind the Creative Subconscious Mind is the **generator** **of** **new** **direc-** **tions**. The Creative Subconscious comes into play when you are no longer satisfied with your Conscious Reality. You are unhappy, depressed, worried, and filled with discontent about where you are in your life. You truly desire a change in your Conscious Reality. Life has dealt you a poor hand and you no longer want to accept it as your lot in life. For instance, you are in a job or on a career path you dislike, working for a boss you find objectionable, and working in an organization whose values are incompatible with yours. You can change all of this through reprogramming your Conscious Mind, and by claiming ownership over the **force within you** [Subconscious Mind]. **To claim ownership, you must activate your Creative Subconscious.**

Here's how your Creative Subconscious works. When your experiences in your Conscious Reality (poor, hungry, abused, etc.) prompts you to be dissatisfied with where you are and you want a different result, it creates a process for you to achieve a new reality. First, it acts upon those unfulfilled hopes and dreams that you desire. The Creative Subconscious is an opportunity for you to acquire new information that take your unrealized hopes and dreams and create a <u>new vision</u> of you pursuing what you want to specifically achieve. This may be a new career or a new set of behaviors. The bottom-line is it will create in your Conscious Reality new behavior(s). Further, it will set in motion the dynamics and experiences that result in new ideas, beliefs, and thoughts and send them to your Conscious Mind. Next, this new information will be sent to the Subconscious Mind to **release the force within you**. Once accepted as truth in the Subconscious Mind you will be placed on automatic pilot for achieving your new hopes, dreams, and goals. The negative behaviors, thoughts, beliefs, attitudes, and values will be replaced with positive ones that support the achievement of your desired goals.

Balance Between the Minds

As we change based on new information, ideas, and practices the picture held in the Conscious and Subconscious Mind must match, because it is impossible to hold one picture in the Conscious Mind and another in the Subconscious Mind and achieve a positive result. Remember that the picture that is held in the Subconscious Mind will always be the controller of the outcome. So, to ensure that you will have positive success in realizing hopes and dreams you must create a positive picture in the Conscious Mind that creates a positive picture in the Subconscious Mind.

By now, we trust that you are eager to learn how to activate your Creative Subconscious to bring about new truths to the Subconscious Mind. In the following chapters, we will introduce to some and reintroduce to others Power Steps: 10 Principles of Success. Individuals who have used these 10 principles, which are: vision, belief, confidence, concentration, competence, energy, enthusiasm, self-talk, spirituality, and action have found a pathway to success.

TWO

VISION

Without a vision of your desired future
any destination will suffice.
——Percy W. Thomas

A purpose driven Vision is the 1st step that must be created to establish how we begin functioning and changing in our Conscious Reality.

Let's look at how Viktor Frankl used the force within him to create a compelling vision that allowed him to survive the German concentration camps, where he was imprisoned. Viktor was born in Vienna on March 26, 1905. He was the middle child of three children. He was an intellectual and very curious about his surroundings and life in general. At age four, he knew he wanted to be a medical doctor, and his High School experiences helped him develop an interest in people, which led him to pursue psychology.

Victor Frankl was without question a man of great intellect and curiosity. However, it is not his intellect that attracted us to include his story in this book. It is how he used his mind under the most extreme inhumane treatment to create a <u>vision</u> that enabled him to cope and live. Through the telling of this short story, we hope to bring more relevance to the great <u>force within</u> each of us to create a vision to determine our future no matter what circumstances we find ourselves in.

In 1942, Victor was arrested along with his brother and mother and placed in a concentration camp. He was separated from his wife when he was arrested, and he had no idea where she was or if she was alive. His mother and brother were killed in 1944, while imprisoned at the Auschwitz Concentration Camp. Victor was starved and treated very badly. It would not have been a surprise to most people if he had died under the conditions in which he was forced to live, but Victor was able to draw on his supernatural power (the force within) to ward off death and stay alive. What supernatural power did he possess? The same power that we all have, the Subconscious Mind, which is <u>the force within</u>. Deep in his Subconscious Mind Victor saw and believed he was a free man and that no matter how he was treated he would remain free in his mind. Victor knew that external forces could change his living conditions, but they could not change the state of his mind. Victor's attitude, beliefs, values, and visions belonged to him and him alone. He could enjoy the fact that whatever he believed and saw in his mind's eye (mental picture) could never be taken away from him. His astute observations of the people who were dying most often in the camps were people who seemingly had nothing to live for.

Victor's Conscious Mind was focused solely on living. Thus, the message to his Subconscious Mind was I am living through this situation. Once the message was recorded in the Subconscious, Victor was placed on an automatic path to survive his captors. The Subconscious supplied him with thoughts of his wife whom he loved. He filled his Conscious Mind with thoughts of seeing his wife, which the Subconscious Mind responded affirmatively. We can imagine that Victor held a clear picture in his Subconscious Mind of him being reunited with his wife. Victor knew intuitively by holding a picture of his wife in his Subconscious it would give him a compelling reason to endure the horrible conditions he faced.

The Mind's Eye

Victor's story demonstrates how your vision can cause you to behave differently in your Conscious Realty.

Many people believe that you see with your eyes, but we have learned over the years that we do not see with our eyes, rather we see with our minds. How is seeing with our mind possible when we have been taught from early childhood that we see with our eyes? In 2 Corinthians 5:7, Paul tells us that as Christians, *"we walk by faith and not by sight."* We recall hearing that scripture in church when we were very young and tried to remember what it meant to us as children; we had to admit that then we didn't have a clue. It was impossible for us to understand how a blind person could walk anywhere without assistance. Today, the meaning of that scripture, as it relates to the power of the Subconscious Mind, makes it clear that we don't see with our eyes; rather, we see by what is stored as our truth in the Subconscious Mind.

This point was driven home for us by observing and assisting a blind person on a subway platform who had lost his bearing in locating the elevators. After giving him directions, Percy asked if he needed help getting there, he said "no I can see my way from here." It was much later, after we had learned that we don't see with our eyes, and that we see with our minds that we came to the understanding of what the blind man's comment meant. He was able to see because after he knew where he was in relation to the elevators, he held a picture in his mind of how to get to the eleva-tors and complete the rest of his journey. The blind man was able to see the elevators and the rest of the way to his destination because he had been taught how to get there.

The experience with the blind man helped us understand the scripture "we walk by faith and not by sight." Our sight is the result of our prior conditioning. We all use our eyes for determining images, however, until we have been taught to assign meaning to the image we take in with our eyes what we see is just an unexplained image. Take for instance as a baby you drank out of a bottle. Imagine what you would have called that bottle if your caretakers never gave you a name for the bottle. What if the caretaker had named the bottle an Elephant, what would you then see when a bottle is presented to you? You would have no choice but to see an Elephant. So, seeing is also a matter of cultural conditioning and learning. Without culture, and without the precondition aspects of culture, we would have no way of labeling things in our current environment, or ways of communicating beyond the level of our domestic animals.

Publilius Syrus a Syrian slave and a Latin writer was correct when he wrote these words *"The eyes are not responsible when the mind does the seeing."*

What Is Vision?

Vision is seeing with the mind's eye a future reality as if it already exists in the present. Whether applied to an individual, group, or an organization, a vision is

Proverbs 29:18
"Where there is no vision, the people perish."

a macro statement or choice about a future state. When referring to vision, we are referencing holding a successful view of the future state, as if it has already occurred in the present. The first principle of success is vision. All success is an outgrowth of a vision that is followed by daily practices that lead to the realization of the vision. John F. Kennedy had a vision when he made the statement that America would place a man on the moon within the 20th century. The actions that many people in this country took after he made that statement were all directed at making his vision a reality. Many people hearing the term vision expressed as a principle tend to discount it and take it as a cliché or a figure of speech. We ask, where would you be in your life today with no vision? It is a simple fact that we all operate from our visions whether we are aware of them or not.

Vision of the Future

A positive vision of the future is the most powerful motivator we can have. Think about where you are in your life at this moment. Perhaps you are at a bank, in a classroom, at home watching television, managing your own business, at church, in the arms of a loved one, married, dating a significant other, or reading this book. Stop and ask yourself how you came to do what you are doing right now. What you may not realize is that you could not do the things you are doing without first seeing yourself doing it.

Creating a vision is the most important thing you can do to become successful in anything that you desire to achieve in life. Whether you create a vision for success or a vision for failure, humans pursue their visions consciously and subconsciously. So why not create a vision for success? The most fundamental thing that you can do to assure your success is to create a vision of your being successful. Create a successful vision of a product to be sold, a happy relationship, a vision of having money, a vision of a great nation, a vision of peace, or a vision of a world without poverty.

Many people who have heard us speak often tell us that they created a vision that worked for them, but they are not happy. When asked to tell us about their vision, they usually say they visualized getting a job or paying specific bills. Immediately, we see what they have done wrong. They have created a very limited and narrowly focused vision. By creating and realizing a vision of getting a job, what have they accomplished?

They have the job and are still poor and unhappy. Their first inclination will be to say the principle of creating a vision does not work. The truth of the matter is the principle worked very well because they got a job. The real problem lies within the quality and specificity of the vision. So what was wrong with the vision? The vision was not specific enough to produce the desired result they really wanted. This is why we caution people to take the time to be clear and specific about what they visualize. In this case, the person visualized getting a job to pay bills. This vision was insufficient and it didn't address what the person really wanted. The Conscious Mind and the Subconscious Mind cannot decipher your unexpressed desires. It receives only what you state. In the vision statement above had the individual stated that they wanted a job within thirty days, that paid eighty five thousand dollars annually, that they enjoyed doing, and that was in an environment that made them happy, the outcome would have been more of what they really wanted. Perhaps, you are wondering why you have to be so specific in creating a vision. It's because you want to bombard your Conscious Mind with an accurate picture of what you see for yourself before it passes to the Subconscious Mind. If your vision lacks specificity, chances are your Subconscious Mind will generate imperfect results that will leave you dissatisfied and unhappy. Remember any vision that reaches your Subconscious will produce an outcome. That is why we ask you to take extra caution when creating a vision.

The creation of your vision must be taken seriously. A vision has great power when it stretches beyond the boundaries of what you know you can already do. We think it is of primary importance for you to be aware that your vision must have some rational truth, in other words, capable of being accomplished. For some people, the importance of holding a clear vision is the key to success. However, we know that the subconscious vision is the one that holds the greatest benefit; since the Subconscious Mind is the reservoir of all motivation, creativity, drive, and energy. If the vision you hold is clear, but superficial because you are not doing anything to make it a reality it will never get to the Subconscious Mind where all true visions must reside.

The Force Within

We have established that the force within is your Subconscious Mind. To release the force within you must create a compelling vision of what you want and know that it is possible to have. Since the Force Within is programmed by the Conscious Mind, the things we want in life can be created. We have the power to create our future through acknowledging that it is all possible. We do it anyway naturally! Think about any of the bad habits we have acquired and that have led us down an unsuccessful path. Didn't we think ourselves into doing those unsuccessful behaviors? Take for example smokers, they know that cigarettes are dangerous and unhealthy, and they know all the negative possibilities associated with smoking. Yet, the smoker chooses to pursue the possibility of living an unhealthy lifestyle and the complications associated with it versus pursuing the possibilities of a healthy lifestyle.

What's the difference in the smoker and nonsmoker? The smoker has the vision of smoking in his Conscious Mind and passes it on to the Force Within (Subconscious Mind) that accepts the vision of being a smoker as truth. It's as though the smoker has no control over smoking. All the facts and conditions possible are in play, therefore, they have no other choice but to smoke.

On the other hand, the nonsmoker does the exact same thing with the exception that his conscious thoughts are of the possibilities associated with a healthy lifestyle. Thus, the Conscious Mind passes on to the Force Within (Subconscious Mind) a vision for living healthy. The Force Within makes possible a vision of health in the nonsmoker and places the individual on a trajectory to achieve a healthy status without smoking. The nonsmoker will see and avail him or herself to all the possibilities to sustain good health.

Without a vision, it is doubtful that any one person or

group of people can be successful in accomplishing anything; nor will they influence others to assist them in achieving their goals. A significant vision precedes significant success. Think about what we just wrote and see if you can think of any one event or person that has been successful without first being associated with a significant picture of what is to be. Think of anyone that has achieved any dream before opening their minds up to what is possible. I don't think you can come up with an example. We have been querying people for years to come up with one. To date we have not found one person. You must have a positive vision of the future in order to see what is possible and to survive and thrive.

We only have to look at Nelson Mandela and Victor Frankel to see two examples of the power of a vision and using the force within to survive. A vision sustained Nelson Mandela for 27 years in prison and Victor Frankel in a Nazi concentration camp through all kinds of threats, trials, and adversity. Ultimately, it was their vision that brought them out of their wretched conditions. In the case of Mandela, he accomplished a supreme victory by becoming free and president of the country that had imprisoned him, South Africa. Victor Frankel's vision allowed him to draw the incredible energy necessary to survive the World War II (WWII) concentration camps and later captured the experience in his book, *Man's Search for Meaning*[2].

---

2   *Man's Search for Meaning, Victor Frankel*

We have just covered the first principle in **Power Steps** and some of you may be thinking: "Is this all that is needed to be successful?" The answer is No! For your vision to be sustained, it needs to be powered by the second principle of *belief.* A vision without belief is like a car without fuel.

THREE

BELIEF

What is a belief? A belief is the mental acceptance that something is true. In this book, a belief is the mental acceptance that your vision is true even though there may be an absence of absolute proof of its external existence. A belief only has to be true for you in order for you to act upon it. According to Maxi Maultsby, all people *"act in accordance with their beliefs and not the objective truth, but the truth as they perceive it or believe it to be."*

Maultsby defines belief as a semi-permanent mental unit that will cause you to take action without the occurrence of an external event. In other words, just by thinking and believing in something strong enough will cause you to take action. This is why we think it is so important that you connect your beliefs to the achievement of your vision.

You must think about your vision in such a way that indicates you believe your vision has already come true. We know that many of you who have been following along with us up to this point are perhaps saying to yourselves that we are talking crazy. Trust me, we are not crazy. It sounds that way to you because you have not been taught the full principle of belief and its power. Nothing that you see around you has come into being without the benefit of thought represented through the beliefs that we hold. Look around you and ask the question, "How did this come to be?" Ask this question about any object that is in your view. We suspect that you will come away with this answer: Everything that I see represents someone's thoughts and beliefs.

Beliefs are fundamental to achievement. Beliefs allow you to claim your success before it happens. This principle works on the simple fact that anything you believe you can achieve. Moreover, anything that you think about you will move toward. Believing in your vision will put you on automatic pilot to achieve it. Many people labor under the mistaken belief that hard work alone will cause you to be successful in making your vision a reality. Hard work plays a part in the process but it is the firm belief that you will do everything that is necessary for success that will make your vision a reality. Successful people throughout history have succeeded through the power of their beliefs. Their beliefs caused them to act in a positive way to support their vision. So the hard work that they did is really the result of their beliefs.

In your Subconscious Mind, beliefs aggregate to form a true picture of your values and that which you will become. Another way of looking at your Subconscious Mind is to view it as the engine of a plane and beliefs as the fuel. Working together, they get the plane to its destination which is the vision. You are probably thinking that I have missed something. How do you get the Subconscious Mind to do all of what you have described is the question you are probably asking yourself. If so, that is a good question and you are following us well.

Through your Conscious Mind your beliefs program your Subconscious Mind to make your dreams and visions come true. Your Conscious Mind has the responsibility to regulate and evaluate your thoughts and beliefs. So any belief that you hold on the conscious level gets communicated to your Subconscious Mind. Therefore, it becomes real important how you evaluate your beliefs on a conscious level. If you are halfhearted about your beliefs, they will become half-hearted truths in the Subconscious Mind. Once beliefs have been accepted as truths in the subconscious, you move towards it on the conscious level without ever really thinking about what you are doing.

"Man is what he believes"said Anton Chekhov[3], a Russian writer, and director. Percy stated he could relate to this statement through his experiences as an athlete, and one particular situation sticks out in his mind. It was in the early '60s and he was a member of the Baltimore Rams football team, as one of two quarterbacks. They were playing for the league championship against the vaunted Omicron Eagles. He was on the bench because he had been in a car accident and had a sprained neck. Up until the fourth quarter of the game he was in pain and could barely turn his head. His body was racked with pain every time he moved his head. The game ended in a tie, and they were now playing in sudden-death overtime. His team had the ball at midfield when a thought entered his head: *"I can win this game for the team."* The next thing that happened surprised everyone. He took off his neck brace and ran to the coach and told him that he wanted to go into the game. The coach looked at him strangely and to this day he cannot tell you what he saw in his eyes or heard in the tone of his voice, but he sent Percy in on third down and long yardage. Percy completed a pass but it was not enough for the first down. However, on fourth down, with 20 yards to go for the first down, and time running out, he threw a 50-yard pass for a touchdown to Isaiah McKenzie. Isaiah, a sure-handed wide receiver caught the ball in the back of the end zone with no room to spare. The Rams won the game!

---

3   Anton Chekhov

Percy professes that it is experiences like this that have caused him to believe and apply Chekhov's philosophy in his life, "if you believe it, you can achieve it."

If You Believe It, You Can Achieve It— But What Happened?

How often have you been introduced to an idea or an activity that excited you? Once hearing about it or experiencing a bit of it, you were gung ho to get started. You jumped in with great gusto and communicated to anyone who would listen your beliefs about it. The picture was very clear in your mind's eye and all your beliefs supported your initial movement to accomplish what you set out to do. As time passed, your enthusiasm waned and you slowly stopped pursuing your goal. Perhaps, you passed off your disengagement as merely no longer having an interest in the goal. Or in some cases people say, they just changed their minds. Your excuses may be right on target, however, it could be that you simply stopped believing it was what you wanted. It is alright for you to change your mind if that is truly what you want to do. However, many people stop pursuing goals they really want because they stop believing that they can realize them.

We want you to know that once you have invested in creating a dynamic vision that your work is not complete. In order for you to realize your vision you will have to support it with strong positive beliefs. Your beliefs undergird your vision and ensures that you will keep moving daily toward your goal. It is important that you monitor everyday what you believe in as it relates to your vision or goal. If you hold negative beliefs they will delay or stop your goal attainment. If your beliefs are positive they will speed up or enhance your goal attainment.

Think about how many times you have been in conversation with someone who has a project they are working on and most of their expressed thoughts about the project are negative. Without being around to see the outcome, I bet you they did not do a good job, or worse they abandoned the project. Are you wondering how we can make this statement? It's because we know negative behaviors follow negative beliefs. If we see negative behavior, we are one hundred percent sure that it is supported by a negative belief.

Let me caution you on a very important aspect of negative and positive beliefs and the people that hold them. Negative thinking and beliefs attract negative people that support negative behavior. Positive thinking and beliefs attract positive people that support positive behavior. Yes, we are definitely advising you to only associate with people who hold positive beliefs about you and your goals. We want you to associate with people who are positive thinkers and likely to give you constructive input. Negative people articulating negative beliefs are likely to infect you and your positive belief system. Last thing you need is a contagion of negativity interrupting your pursuit of your vision and goals.

Reframing Negative Beliefs

Beliefs are the source of your thoughts and are the instruments by which you program your Subconscious Mind. Thus, they are very powerful and important to your success. Since beliefs can be positive or negative, you need to be prepared to handle both types of beliefs. Despite what we have said about why you should stay clear of negative people who hold negative beliefs, we know unless you are a hermit, it will be difficult for you not to encounter negative people.

Negative beliefs must be reframed when they seep into your belief system and positive beliefs need to be reinforced. You are now thinking why do I need to know about reinforcing and reframing beliefs to be successful? Your beliefs are a public declaration of your expected outcomes; therefore they must be precise, accurate and positive. They also reflect the knowledge, and philosophy you hold about your vision. Simply put your beliefs initiate your behaviors. You must charge your vision with your beliefs because your deeply held beliefs are a statement of your values. Your values are an aggregate of beliefs that go unquestioned. Once they are in your Subconscious Mind they are there until you replace them with beliefs of equal value.

Think about this for a minute. If negative beliefs creep into your Subconscious Mind they remain there influencing all sorts of negative behaviors sending you down a life path of failure and discontent. So how do you get them out? You must turn those negative beliefs into positive or rational beliefs that produce positive behavior moving on the path of goal attainment. You must reframe your negative beliefs (which are negative thoughts).

Before we go any further, I want you to repeat the following statements aloud:

1. My thoughts are created from my beliefs.
2. My beliefs trigger my behavior and emotions.
3. I control my thoughts and thus, I control my emotions.
4. The positive or negative things that happen to me are the result of my thoughts unless it is done to me by force.
5. I can change my unwanted beliefs/thoughts by reframing them

We have borrowed the concepts of the ABC Model of Rational Thinking and Emotional Self Control from Maxi C. Maultsby, Jr. and Albert Ellis to create the **ABC Model of Reframing Beliefs**.

A. Event/Situation (Vision)

B. Your evaluative thoughts about events/situation (beliefs)
   A & B = Your habitually paired beliefs

C. Your emotions, feelings/behavior (actions)
   C = Emotions, feelings/behavior (actions)

In this model, you are made aware of how your vision, which in the model is how the <u>event/situation</u> is affected by your <u>evaluative thoughts</u>, which becomes your beliefs and how the two working together affect your <u>actions</u>/behaviors.

Example:

If you are a student and your vision is to be a brain surgeon, but your evaluative thoughts are that you are stupid, dumb, and incapable of being a brain surgeon, then you will take actions, like failing tests, missing key classes, and not completing assignments to act in accordance with your evaluative thoughts/beliefs. What you see in this example is how negative thoughts/beliefs predispose an individual to negative behavior. To change the negative behavior you must reframe the evaluative thoughts and beliefs that you hold about the event/situation. Negative thoughts/beliefs must be changed to: I will pass the test with flying colors, attend all scheduled classes, and complete all assignments on time, in order for positive behavior to occur.

This is why and how you can reframe your thoughts and beliefs.

You still may have one lingering question about reframing beliefs and it is how do I know when my belief(s) need to be reframed? That is easy to answer. When they produce behavior that distracts you from achieving your vision, goals and projects.

Reinforcing Positive Beliefs

When you least expect it a positive thought will enter your Conscious Mind that relates to your vision, goals or project. It may have come from your interactions with associates that believe in what you are doing or share your vision. It really doesn't matter where the thoughts come from as long as they are positive and move you toward your desired outcome. Don't spend any time on trying to figure out where the belief came from, it would be simply an exercise in futility. Human beings are bombarded with millions of ideas, thoughts, and beliefs that vibrate constantly in their environment as they go about their daily lives. What you need to be able to do is recognize and reinforce positive beliefs when they surface.

Reinforcing positive beliefs strengthen your resolve to realize your vision or goals. We recommend three time tested steps to reinforce positive thoughts and the beliefs you hold:

1. Put your positive beliefs in writing and read them three times a day. This will help you to readily accept new positive ideas and thoughts when you hear them.
2. Pray and meditate about what you believe.
3. Act daily as if your beliefs have already come true.

To ensure that you are clear about beliefs that need to be reframed and those that need to be reinforced, just keep in mind that any message sent to you that indicates you "can't" or are "lacking" in any way needs to be reframed with a different message.

As we close our discussion of beliefs keep the following statements in mind.

1. Beliefs lead you to success or failure.
2. Beliefs produce behavior.
3. If you believe it you can achieve it.

Now that you understand the importance of having a clear vision and anchoring it with unshakeable beliefs, in the following chapters, we will share with you how the remaining principles help you to use your Creative Subconscious Mind to change.

FOUR

THREE C'S: COMPETENCE, CONCENTRATION, CONFIDENCE

While we know that if you can master an understanding of how the Mind works, create a vision of what you desire, and sustain it with beliefs you will be successful in achieving your goals, the following principles serve as the core that makes you a better person and keeps you evolving and growing in your search for excellence. They are the steps needed to activate your Creative Subconscious Mind so that you **can** and **will** embrace new ideas to move in a new direction.

Chapter Four begins the discussion of what we have come to refer to as the "Three C's": Competence, Concentration, and Confidence. In the book, <u>Power</u>

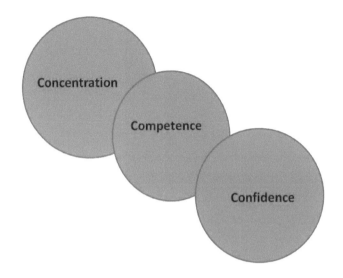

Steps: 10 Principles of Success, each of these principles were given a dedicated chapter, but as we presented the concepts at workshops and seminars it became clear to us that it was important to link them together. In fact, we began to recognize the weight and strength that each principle contained. Visualize the concepts associated with our Model of the Mind and the 10 Principles in a gym as weights. We see the Mind as the 100 lb. weight in the room next to it is Vision as the 90 lb. weight, and Belief as the 80 lb. weight followed by the remaining principles at 25 lbs. each. This difference in weight size is intended to demonstrate the importance of understanding the concepts of the Mind, Vision, and Belief and to make it clear how the remaining principles contribute to Power Steps to keep you balanced in order to achieve success. The lack of anyone of these principles will have an impact on the total model, skew your results, and potentially derail you.

Competence is being sufficiently prepared both,
physically and mentally, to perform at a level of excellence.
—Percy W. Thomas

When thinking of success for ourselves we must always consider competence. For, without competence, there is little we will be able to accomplish. Competence supports vision and beliefs, like a radar screen supports the captain of a ship who has the responsibility to direct a ship to a destination. In this case, the captain has to have skill and knowledge to read the radar screen to ensure that the goal will be reached. Without competence in the appropriate areas, the captain may fail. So, you may have a clear vision, fueled by strong beliefs, however, without a measure of competence you will be unable to succeed.

So what is competence? Competence is the knowledge and skill required to be successful in any endeavor that you choose to pursue. When we think of someone being competent, what picture do we see in our mind's eye? It is usually, someone we view as having some special knowledge, skill, or ability in a particular field, or it could be a special experience. The *Random House Dictionary of The English Language* defines competence as "the quality of being competent; the possession of a required skill, knowledge, qualification, or capacity."

Competence has to do with your capability to achieve your vision and move toward that which you believe. Competence suggests capability. When you have a belief it is not enough to expect that your belief will just come true without you taking an active role in making it happen.

Barbara Jordan said it best, *"If you're going to play the game properly, you'd better know every rule."* We take Barbara Jordan's words to mean that you had better prepare yourself for the battle and become competent and multi-talented. This means that you must become a lifelong learner. School is never out or over until your life has ended. We live in a country where importance is placed on the quality and quantity of what you know. In America, knowledge is power. Knowledge translates into competency should you have the desire and confidence to use it. Therefore, anyone who visualizes success in their life must also make a commitment to become competent in their field.

On a more general level, competence in modern times means constant learning for coping with the myriad of fast-paced changes in life. The rationale for this constant learning stems from the fact that technology and information change at an alarming pace in today's world. How do we constantly learn? The answer, for starters, is by reading everything we can get our hands on. And for sure, by reading everything that pertains to the area in which we are striving to be successful. Are you aware, that any subject that you read and study for one year you will amass great knowledge and competency? It seems like hard work and it is, but it is well worth it.

Think a little deeper about the expression that *"knowledge is power?"* Well, competence is also perceived as power. Think about the power that lawyers, accountants, and doctors possess. They have the knowledge, and in most instances, the skill to influence others' outcomes and behaviors.

Over the years, we have become aware that sometimes your competence is based on what you know, who you know or in the case of the professionals noted above sometimes by the perceptions of the degrees you hold. Alice remembers that after she retired from the federal government as an executive in charge of a multi-billion dollar grant and contract program, she went to work for a small college. Until then, her Master's Degree in Applied Behavioral Science with a concentration in Organizational Development from Johns Hopkins University had served her well. She quickly discovered, however, that unless you were being referred to as "doctor," the acceptance or validity of what she said was questioned and often dismissed. Having been an executive for over 25 years, she was unwilling to accept this status. The vision she created for herself was to go back to school to earn a Ph.D., as quickly as possible. Three years later, she returned to the same college as Alice Thomas, Ph.D. and received a different reception. Her area of expertise was in the area of grants and contracts, which is what she knew before she left, but with a doctoral degree she was perceived as more competent. In achieving ones goals and fulfilling ones vision, it is important to determine what level of competence is required to be successful.

Concentration has to do with one's ability
to pay attention and focus on what is important.
—Percy W. Thomas

What Is Concentration?

Concentration involves one's ability to focus on a task. In terms of Power Steps, it is the complete application of self to accomplish the task. In this chapter, we are using concentration and focus as interchangeable words. To be successful in life, at times one must harness personal power in order to concentrate. In further expressing how concentration relates to the principles, we define it as "the capability to direct one's thoughts toward their vision and beliefs." The key here is that, by concentrating our thoughts on believing our vision can be achieved, we block out all distractions that would prevent us from realizing our vision.

Focused Attention

When referring to attention in Power Steps, we are talking about the selective aspects of perception, which are natural ways in which people see things in the environment. In short, it is paying attention to what is important in your environment at the time. Thus, attention may be considered a general term referring to the selective aspects of perceptions which function so that a person can pay attention to certain aspects of the environment to the exclusion of other aspects. When individuals experience this phenomenon in their daily encounters, they have a "scotoma." For example, have you ever found yourself driving on the expressway when you were in deep thought, and then not remembering how you got to your destination? Your experience was the result of a scotoma.

A scotoma serves a vital purpose in support of concentration and paying close attention to what is important in your life. They allow you to block out distractions for specified periods so you can concentrate on what needs to be accomplished. At the "Investment in Excellence Conference that we attended in Seattle, Washington, we can remember Lou Tice calling this the "Lock-on / Lock-out" approach.

You Can Learn to Concentrate

Most human beings have the ability to focus their attention at various times. However, many are unable to concentrate at the times when it counts. Perhaps we can all relate to a work situation, school project, or personal commitment requiring us to concentrate, but we could not maintain the required level of attention. Our thoughts were scattered all over the place and our mind jumped from one point to another, leaving us feeling frustrated. It is times like these that we need to know how to build a scotoma to activate the principle of concentration, because this is precisely when we need to be able to focus. Therefore, we need to have in our human success tool bag strategies and techniques to enable us to concentrate instantly.

Perhaps you are wondering if we are suggesting that concentration is a learned skill. In fact, I am emphatically saying that **you can learn to concentrate**, whenever you choose, at any time, and in any place. To do so, you must first learn to focus on your vision and associated beliefs. Since concentration is a learned skill, this means making real the old adage, "practice makes perfect." We must practice repeatedly day after day until we are able to turn our ability to concentrate on and off like a water faucet.

Keys to Concentration

Our ability to concentrate depends on four keys: motivation, enthusiasm, energy, and attitude. These four keys must be directed toward achieving the vision we set in our mind's eye. Thus, concentration is a matter of mindset supported by the consistent human behavior of employing the four keys that lead to a capacity to focus on what is important. Further, it is the conscious effort to use the four keys that strengthen the innate human capacity for concentration, which we acquire at birth, and use throughout our lives. Think about the example of driving to a destination while you were in deep thought and arriving without remembering how you got there. If this has ever happened to you, our point has been made that the ability to concentrate is a natural part of your biological makeup and an innate skill set in the human arsenal of success behaviors.

Many people give themselves negative messages regarding their ability to concentrate. We have heard people, when frustrated by a task, say, "I can't concentrate." With such a message programmed into their Subconscious Minds, it is not surprising that they believe they can't concentrate. So, the first hurdle one must overcome in developing the ability to concentrate is to stop programming your mind to believe that you can't concentrate. Remember that we act in accordance with our beliefs, and if we believe we cannot do something then it would be incongruous to do it.

The caution here is that we must be careful of the messages we give ourselves regarding what we can and cannot do in general and, in this instance, specifically as it relates to our ability to concentrate.

Concentration is a State of Mind

Concentration is an essential state of mind if you want to be consistently successful in nearly anything you wish to accomplish. The mind is a vessel and the negative thoughts contained in it, regarding concentration, are a major barrier to being able to concentrate instantly and consistently. When most of us incorrectly perceive our inability to concentrate, we are really worrying about our ability to do the task, versus concentrating on how to complete the job. The more you think or worry about not being able to complete the task, the less you will focus on your ability to concentrate. Your inability to concentrate on a specific activity acts as a saboteur of your ability to get the job done. To eliminate this problem, We suggest you focus on creating a vision for how the job will look when it is successfully completed and identify five associated beliefs related to the vision. Then set aside time to focus on the vision and the five beliefs. This indirect strategy should enable you to improve concentration and move toward achieving the results you desire. This strategy in Power Steps is referred to as the "Indirect Focus Approach." By focusing on what the task will look like when it is successfully finished and the be-liefs associated with its success, the focus is taken off of your inability to concentrate on the problem, thus eliminating barriers, harmful worrying, and the intrusion of unwelcome distractions.

Barriers to Concentration

The main barriers to concentrating are irrational thinking, distractions, worry, and fear. Thus, in improving our concentration skills we need to develop a rational way to look at and handle these barriers. The following five skills are basic to concentration:

1. Create a vision of what you want to achieve
2. Write five core beliefs to support achieving the vision
3. Write an action plan with a timeline to achieve the vision
4. Set aside a specific time to work on a plan
5. Practice mentally going through the first four skills three times a day for five minutes each time. (The point here is that, if you want to improve your concentration, you must practice, practice, and practice.)

Concentration has to do with one's ability to pay attention and focus on what is important. In Power Steps, concentration is an essential element to reaching your vision, activating positive beliefs, and executing your competencies. Concentration and focus are synonymous terms which trigger scotomas that block out distractions so that individuals can successfully complete tasks, and reach their goals. To make concentration work you must devise ways to practice, practice, and practice frequently. Successful concentration builds **confidence**.

What is Confidence?

As a young boy of nine years old, Percy sought the answer to this question because it was then that he first became aware of the emotion of fear inside of him. Even now, he can remembers vividly how afraid he was of the boys who lived in his East Baltimore neighborhood. They were more streetwise and tougher. His mother told him to develop confidence in himself and she made Percy go outside and mingle with the boys who eventually became his friends. Thus, for him, confidence meant developing a belief that he could do something that he was afraid of doing.

There are many ways to look at confidence. In Power Steps, *confidence is an aggregate of beliefs held about one's abilities to cope automatically with any situation in life with trust and certitude.* Thus, confidence is also an attitude of self-assurance, trust, certitude, and a strong belief in one's ability to be successful in dealing with people of all ages, ethnic origins, cultural orientations, and different personalities.

Confidence is a Lifestyle

Confidence is a lifestyle because it is a way of being and acting which enables you to take on the most difficult tasks in life with aplomb. Confidence as a human characteristic influences how others see you and the level of faith and trust they will place in you. I can't imagine a situation that you will find yourself in where you will not need to be confident. Whether you are praying, skiing, rollerblading, giving a speech, baking a cake, planning an event, or interviewing for a job, you will need to have confidence. Since confidence or the lack of it is related to everything you do in life, why not make a conscious effort to be confident by taking on the challenges of living in a complex world with gusto and enthusiasm? By making confidence part of your lifestyle behavior, you increase your opportunities to become a leader.

Confidence is a Leadership Trait

When you think of a leader, you probably think of someone guiding, directing, and commanding an activity or a group. From an authoritarian perspective, perhaps you think of an individual in charge. None of you perceive a leader to be weak, lacking the ability to give direction, and without a vision or plan for the activity or group. Confidence is a trait expected in successful leaders.

Great leaders must model the way to perform and confidence must rank high as a trait they must possess. We don't believe a leader who lacks confidence in themselves will be able to effectively lead others. Can you imagine a leader influencing you or members of a team you are on to work hard towards achieving a goal without it? How about a teacher who lacks confidence in the subject matter he/she is teaching? How would you respond to such a teacher? Further, we believe part of the leader's role is to instill their leadership traits into the groups they lead. If a leader wants a confident team, he/she must have those characteristics and live them in a visible manner. In essence, a leader must lead by example and this means displaying confidence in every aspect of your life. Thus, leaders must model confidence for their followers, and if they do not possess confidence they must develop it.

Confidence is the Breakfast of Champions

Each day is an opportunity to start out with renewed confidence. In fact, I believe that each day you must feed yourself a dose of affirmations related to your confidence. In other words, feed yourself a breakfast of statements like the following:

- "I am the greatest"
- "I achieve great things"
- "I am smart"
- "People listen and follow me"
- "Nervousness gives me energy to succeed"

Notice that the statements are positive and self-affirming. Self-affirming is the key to your breakfast, because no one else can affirm your success or will you to have confidence. It is something you must do and only you can do for yourself. If you don't feed your soul confidence for breakfast every day, you will never have confidence in yourself nor will you ever take steps to change your circumstances or the world.

Confidence is a Gift

Confidence is also a gift which allows you to live a life without mind-numbing fear, fear that keeps you inert and from being all you can be in a country full of opportunities. Confidence is the catalyst that will project you into the world of possibilities and provide you with the will power to pursue your dreams with faith and deliberateness. There is no point in having a vision and believing in that vision if you don't have the confidence to pursue what you envision and believe in. Thus, each of us owes it to ourselves to further develop the gift of confidence that each of us has been given at birth.

Develop Confidence to Succeed

If confidence is an aggregate of beliefs held about one's abilities to cope with any situation in life with trust and certitude automatically, then how does one develop confidence to succeed in a world where there are so many possibilities to fail? We believe you take one step at a time, one success at a time, and build on each successive step to gain confidence in taking another. To move one step at a time as it relates to confidence requires planning. Therefore, an individual must plan to build their confidence by creating a plan of action that ensures success in achieving small steps. This is the basis for building confidence and long-term success. If you have heard the expression, "you eat an elephant one bite at a time," then you can apply it to building confidence one success at a time.

To build confidence you must be bold in your planning; therefore, the goals in your plans must stretch you a bit. You must choose a goal that captures your mind's eye and automatically drives you to accomplish it successfully with confidence.

Eliminate the Concept of Lack of Confidence

You have no room for the concept of lack of confidence in your thought process and you must strive to extinguish it from your mind. When other people attempt to describe you in *As a young girl, my grandfather would always say, "Never let someone else paint a picture of who you are."* terms of lacking in confidence, reframe it in terms of a goal you are confident you will achieve. Do not let others describe you as lacking in confidence; this is a domain that you and only you should control.

Perceiving a lack of confidence as a debilitating characteristic will ensure failure if allowed to persist as a dominant thought in your mind. Lack of confidence is often associated with embarrassment and blame which can sabotage anyone's self-confidence or progress. Many individuals confuse failure with lack of confidence. When people fail at something they look for a reason for the failure and often they blame it on a lack of confidence in giving it 100% effort. In reality, the failure has nothing to do with lack of confidence; rather it is an unwillingness to try again. I don't believe failure alone creates a sense of lack of confidence, it is failure coupled with the belief in your head that you can't achieve a goal or objective that leads to behavior associated with lack of confidence. The key to confidence is first thinking confident thoughts and behaving in a confident manner.

Practice Confidence

1. Look in the mirror each morning and affirm that you are a confident person who accomplishes everything you put a 100% effort behind.

2. Write your self-confidence affirmation of the day on a 5x7 card and read it three times during the day, six times at each reading.

3. Do not associate or listen to people that lack confidence in themselves because they will project their issues onto you. You will become weighted down with their negative stories of doom and gloom to the point of doubting yourself.

4. Take a few minutes in the morning to review your plans for the day. Make modifications in your daily plans to ensure small successes.

5. Make an effort to teach a friend, coworker or family member something about building and maintaining confidence. We learn best ourselves by what we endeavor to teach others.

6. Assess how well you practiced being confident

during the day. Celebrate your successes by treating yourself to something small that you enjoy or just by giving yourself several verbal accolades for doing a good job. Remember that rewarding yourself for confident behavior increases the chances of your being even more confident in the future.

7. Read a self-help book relating to personal development for 20 minutes before retiring for the night.

Develop an Attitude of Confidence

We learned at an early age that confidence is a mental attitude that involves not trusting in or relying on a person or thing. Remember that an attitude places you on automatic pilot to act when an event or a situation occurs. If you have developed a level of competence in your ability to execute in certain areas of your life and have positive beliefs relative to the person, event or situation you find yourself involved with, more than likely you will act with confidence. To operationalize the principle of confidence, you must first program your Subconscious Mind that you possess a high level of trust, faith, and are without fear regarding the event or situation presented. Once the correlate attitudes of trust, faith, and fearlessness are established in your Subconscious Mind, you will begin to behave with confidence any time you are presented with an event or situation regardless of how much or how little you know about it.

FIVE

ENTHUSIASM

"The habit of being enthusiastic paves the way
to making the impossible, possible."
—*Percy W. Thomas*

The next two weights Enthusiasm and Energy are important to the Creative Subconscious if we are to maintain a commitment to achieving ones goals. First, let's focus on Enthusiasm.

Ralf Waldo Emerson's quote *"Nothing great was ever achieved without enthusiasm"* is the lens we would like reader's to view the Principle of Enthusiasm through. Enthusiasm in Power Steps is one of the weights that support the principles of Vision, and Belief in creating the success you desire. Think about your vision and beliefs for a moment. Your vision is clear and are supported by strong positive beliefs. How do you make manifest your vision and beliefs? This is not a trick question? How you present your vision and beliefs to the world are important. If you present them in a low key lackadaisical way to others what do you think it communicates about you and your vision? If you were presenting yourself to us, we would think you did not believe in your vision, and that you lacked enthusiasm for it. Further, we would not be eager to invest in you or your vision. That might be a bitter pill for you to swallow, however, it is true.

We have talked to many hiring officials who have told us that when they are interviewing a person for a job, they look for enthusiasm in the individual. When two job seekers are nearly equal in talent, education, and skills, they select the one that demonstrates the greatest amount of enthusiasm.

Why does enthusiasm matter you might be asking yourself? The answer is because it reflects your excitement about what you envision and believe. Moreover, it shows your strong interests and commitment to realizing your vision and it is indicative of holding strong beliefs about your pursuit. It is also a way of motivating yourself to stay on course until you have accomplished what you set out to do.

When we decided to write this book we instantly became excited about the idea. We set a goal of writing the book in a week. Now that was a daunting task for sure, however, our enthusiasm kicked in and before we knew it we were telling our children that we were going to take a week and go to the mountains and write a new Power Steps book. Then, we called a friend that owned a vacation home in the mountains of West Virginia and asked if we could use her place. She graciously consented and before we knew it we had moved in with our computers and printers and were off to the races. Each morning we got up energized and full of ideas to write. We wrote all day and late into the night. Not once during our stay did we complain or feel tired. We believed that our enthusiasm for the task sustained us. Our takeaway from our experience is that enthusiasm is a catalyst for <u>energy</u> and <u>action</u>. It is also a magnet that attracts whatever you need. For example, when you develop writers block and at times we did, our enthusiasm for the task activated the **_force within_** us to connect with new ideas about the book and how to proceed. Enthusiasm interacts with the **Sub Conscious Mind** in ways that allowed us to have access to the millions of ideas, beliefs, and concepts it stores.

Here is something about enthusiasm that should get your attention. If your life seems mundane and lacks pep you may have developed a habit of being unenthusiastic about life. If you have, then you may have placed limits on how much success you will have in a job or perhaps in life. The habit of being unenthusiastic may drain your energy for taking on new tasks with excitement in the future. It potentially could open the door to woe is me thinking, which is the kiss of death to success. Now that we have your attention on the importance of enthusiasm to success, let's dive deeper and learn more about enthusiasm as a principle of success.

What is Enthusiasm?

The word "enthusiasm" has a Greek origin and means "God within" (*ethos*). It refers to a spiritual spark or fire that burns within the heart of those with fervor for a cause, job, or life in general. Webster's Dictionary defines enthusiasm as: *1) great excitement for or interest in a subject or cause; or 2) a source or cause of great excitement or interest.* According to Arthur James Balfour, a conservative Prime Minister of Great Britain enthusiasm *"moves the world."* According to Henry Ford, the inventor of the Ford automobile, enthusiasm *"is the yeast that makes your hopes rise to the stars."* In both these quotes from great men, we see enthusiasm as a catalyst for propelling individuals, groups, and systems to a higher level of achievement. From a practical sense enthusiasm may be viewed as the bounce in your step, the twinkle in your eye, the swagger in your walk. Thus, the principle of enthusiasm is critical to achieving success.

Enthusiasm and Great Things

Have you ever been so tired that you felt that if you didn't rest, you would pass out from exhaustion? However, you decided to check your E-mail before retiring and discovered a message from a friend inviting you to a show. They have two tickets to a sold-out play that you wanted to see. In minutes, you are showered, dressed, and on your way to the theater full of energy. What happened to your exhaustion? Where did all that energy come from? Your exhaustion was overcome by your enthusiasm to attend the show. That is an example of the power of enthusiasm. It is a trigger for doing great things in the face of what appears to be impossible barriers. The key is to make enthusiasm a positive habit and practice it in every facet of your life, your job, family, and social setting; to make getting things done seem effortless. The habit of Enthusiasm will not only make you more productive, but it will lighten burdens and make obstacles easier to overcome. With reference to enthusiasm and accomplishing great things, I Ching put it this way *"He who possesses the source of enthusiasm will achieve great things."* Do not doubt this statement for we have observed it to be true in our lives leading us to present ourselves in all situations with enthusiastic presence. If you do things with enthusiasm, you are more likely to be happy and excited about doing it and it will appear effortless to others. This increased energy coupled with your own enthusiasm will also make you happier for, as Charles Kingsley wrote, "We *act as though comfort and luxury were the chief goals of life, when all that we need to make us happy is something to be enthusiastic about.*"

Enthusiasm is Contagious

Enthusiasm is contagious and Percy has been infected with it many times, especially in his passion for the theater. Once he auditioned for a play at the Arena Playhouse in Baltimore, Maryland. Mr. Samuel Wilson, the director of the play, was so enthusiastic about the play **Clara's Old Man** that he could barely remain seated during the audition and first reading. Based on his display of exuberance, everyone auditioning wanted to be a member of the cast or on the production team. Percy was not a very good reader at the time and had not done well in the audition; however, he was invited back for the second reading the next day. To this day, he remembers being so enthusiastic about being asked back for the second reading that he memorized the entire one-act play overnight. He read well during the second reading and was cast in a part. For the next three weeks of rehearsal, all members of the production appeared to eat, sleep, and drink **Clara's Old Man**.

Over the years, Percy's passion for theater has not changed and now he can boast that his daughters, son, grandson and even I have been smitten by some facet of theater. Enthusiasm is contagious, and will produce memorable experiences that sometimes will take your breath away.

On the other hand, a lack of enthusiasm is also contagious and works equally well. At this point, a word of caution is in order for individuals who lack enthusiasm. What if Mr. Wilson had been pessimistic about the play? Perhaps, Percy and others would have caught pessimism rather than enthusiasm. The message here is to be careful of the people you choose to follow and select to be your friends, they may be contagious with pessimism, doom, and gloom. They see the glass half empty versus viewing it as half full. An American author and doctor, David Seabury, once said, *"Enthusiasm is the best protection in any situation. Wholeheartedness is contagious. Give of yourself if you wish to get others."*

Enthusiasm is a Way of Putting Dreams into Action

You can generally tell when the people around you are enthusiastic, because they will have a spring in their step and a glint in their eye, and their stories will have a positive bent, be uplifting, and inspiring. You will find yourself being excited by what they have to say and enjoy being in their presence. John Wesley, the founder of Methodism, summed it up best with regard to the concept and principle of enthusiasm as it relates to its contagious effect on people: *"Catch on fire with enthusiasm and people will come for miles to watch you burn.*" Remember that your enthusiasm will attract others to your projects. Denis Waitley, author, speaker, trainer, and peak performance expert, also described enthusiasm in a similar manner: *"Get excited and enthusiastic about your own dream. This excitement is like a forest fire—you can smell it, taste it, and see it from miles away."*

The principle of Enthusiasm is connected to the principle of Vision in that your vision becomes a repeated dream. By being excited about your vision, you are automatically excited and enthusiastic about your dreams. The point here is to make a conscious effort to be enthusiastic about your dreams. Talk about them with energy and excitement several times a day to affirm them in your Subconscious Mind, and make sure that your body language is congruent with your enthusiasm relative to your dreams.

Enthusiasm is a Way of Communicating

Both verbally and non-verbally, you must communicate with energy and great zest. The way you communicate that which you desire to accomplish will have an impact on whether you achieve your goal. The art of communicating is based on the fundamental steps of sending and receiving messages. Most everyone has the ability to send and receive messages; however, whether the messages are received and understood as intended is another story. When messages are received and not acted upon, one can assume with some degree of certainty that there has been miscommunication. Communicating with enthusiasm helps clarify the message and emphasizes its importance. It increases the potential of the message being received as it was intended and then acted upon.

How do we Cultivate the habit of Enthusiasm?

Begin by being aware. Wake up and appreciate all that you have. What about your beautiful home? I'm not speaking about the apartment or house that you live in, but the universe. We are on a small planet, circling a minor star, which is at the edge of one of a hundred thousand million galaxies. Vast as the universe is, we can contain it within our mind! How incredible we are! Like the universe, we have unlimited potential! Isn't that something to be excited about? Enthusiasm can be an expression of the joy of living.

What about your job? You won't be enthusiastic about it unless you love what you do. If you are unable to find a job that you are passionate about, make the best of the situation. Look for the good and the potential of your present job. Also, make a plan and take action that will lead you to the job of your dreams. It may be a long struggle before you get there but, like climbing a great mountain, you will find the journey exhilarating.

To anchor enthusiasm in your Subconscious Mind you must consciously practice being enthusiastic. In essence, make enthusiasm a habit. We suggest that you document, daily, 10 things you have done to demonstrate your enthusiasm and beside each item indicate whether what you did was communicated with excitement and energy. Three of the 10 things should relate to what we call dropping a light into the soul of another. This means finding something positive to say about someone with whom you have come in contact. To try this, greet at least five people in an enthusiastic manner using the following steps:

1. Look the person you are greeting in the eyes and be warm and friendly.

2. Give a firm handshake but be sure not to squeeze the hand in a vise grip. If you hurt the person's hand you are shaking, you have failed.

3. Offer a warm, personal, and sincere greeting. Find something positive to say. For instance, I am delighted to meet you or I have heard many good things about you or you remind me of ……..; be authentic but be specific.

4. Upon leaving, be sure to repeat the process and give a warm and personal good bye message, such as, "I enjoyed spending time with you and look forward to talking with you again."

Also, write a personal affirmation regarding your being an enthusiastic person and read it daily, twice in the morning and twice before going to bed. Here is an example of a daily Enthusiasm affirmation: "I greet everyone in a warm, friendly manner and with a positive attitude towards them as a human being that has the potential to help me make a difference in the world." You must write your own and live it daily.

> *I am reminded of the words of H.W. Arnold:*
> *"The worst bankruptcy in the world*
> *is the person who has lost his enthusiasm."*

The fact that we all have the capability to reinvent ourselves multiple times over the course of our lifetime makes the prospects of improving ourselves unlimited and therefore electrifying. A sure way to inject some enthusiasm into your life is to read this book, take a few adult education courses, take a trip, learn a new craft, fall in love, or anything else that is positive. The most important thing you can do once you have become enthusiastic is to share your bright outlook with others. Become a giver of light to others through sharing your own zest for life with others.

Consider this statement as we read about the principle of **Energy**. If we as humans become bankrupt in our enthusiasm, it will be very difficult for us to generate the energy to realize our vision.

SIX

ENERGY

*"The force is within every human
to harness the energy, power, and strength
to create what is necessary for succes."*
—Percy W. Thomas

When Percy was a small boy and resisted doing his chores or was slow going about tasks, his mother frequently said, *"Boy, you had better get some energy."* She would also insist that he eat something before going to school, and her favorite words were, *"you need food for energy to help you work"* or *"Food is good for the brain, it gives it energy to think."* His dad, on the other hand, admonished him for his lackadaisical behavior towards tasks by saying, *"You had better put some elbow grease into the job."* He did not realize at the time that his mother and father were teaching a fundamental principle of how to be successful, which was that the ability to do work is dependent upon human energy.

When you are young you don't readily understand the importance of having and maintaining energy to be successful. You have boundless energy to use for everything you decide to do, and you use it without thinking about it. As you mature, energy becomes an important aspect in every facet of your life in moving toward success. It becomes extremely important when you have a vision that you are in pursuit of reaching. Awake or asleep requires an expenditure of energy. The daily activities we take for granted such as brushing our teeth, taking a bath, cooking food, brushing our hair, and pursuing our dreams all require an expenditure of energy.

Energy fuels the body, like beliefs fuel your Conscious and Subconscious Minds. It strengthens the physical body and repairs and heals when there is trauma. It allows us to take on taxing physical tasks and recover from them quickly. Not only does good physical energy enable the body to be strong, it supports the body to have excellent emotional strength. Emotional strength is needed to deal with the myriad of unanticipated challenges you will encounter on your way to success.

The Principle of Energy is perhaps the easiest to understand, and the hardest to apply on a consistent basis.

Judging from the statistics on obesity, lots of people ignore the messages that a nutritious diet is required for optimum energy; however, sustained success is interdependent on maintaining healthy emotional and physical energy.

What is Energy?

The relationship between work, play, and energy is affirmed through our understanding of basic physics. In the context of physics, any system which produces work is considered to possess energy. So "energy is the ability to do work." The amount of energy possessed by a body is equal to the amount of work it can produce when its energy is released. When work is done, energy is used.

There are several important types of energy that exist:

1. Human Energy
   a. Emotional Energy
   b. Mental Energy
   c. Physical Energy
   d. Psychological Energy
   e. Sexual Energy
   f. Spiritual Energy
2. Heat Energy
3. Chemical Energy
4. Electrical Energy

5. Nuclear Energy
6. Solar Energy

The principle of energy in this chapter deals with human energy. Therefore, it is helpful to have a basic understanding in simple terms of what these different forms of energy are about before we proceed:

- **Emotional Energy** is the energy necessary to control our emotions and cope with the stress and conflict associated with achieving success.
- **Mental energy** refers to energy used in thinking, reasoning, and solving of problems.
- **Physical energy** refers to our metabolism and the body's ability to generate energy for autonomous functions, activities, and behaviors. It is associated with general nutrition, diet, exercise, and rest required for the body to generate the appropriate amounts of energy to accomplish work.
- **Psychological energy** refers to enthusiasm, drive, and resilience. It is associated with the beliefs, attitudes, and values that we hold in our Subconscious Mind. The Subconscious Mind creates the appropriate mental paradigm that produces mental energy to maintain a high social and emotional intelligence necessary to sustain mental toughness related to being successful.
- **Sexual energy** refers to the primal urge to procreate.

- **Social Energy** is related to the required energy necessary to build and maintain effective relationships with others. This energy is necessary to build partnerships and work in teams as it relates to accomplishing goals.
- **Spiritual energy** refers to the ability to have faith in a higher power greater than oneself and the belief that the power is accessible.

Energy that produces higher temperatures is called heat energy. The energy produced by a chemical reaction is called chemical energy. The energy of an electric current is called electrical energy. The energy produced by fission or fusion of the nucleus of an atom is called nuclear energy. The energy radiated by the sun is called solar energy. Notice that each energy source has a common element of power and force. Also note that each energy source cited is related to making something happen.

In our society, we associate each energy source with the ability, power, and force to do work. When we speak of power and force as it relates to energy, we are referring to the power and force within all humans to accomplish work successfully. So, when we refer to the **force within**, we are speaking of the human capability and capacity to generate energy to be successful in any life endeavor of one's choosing.

The Force Within

We believe that each one of us is created with a *force within* which generates energy. The *force within* each of us that is generating energy is our **Mind** (Conscious and Subconscious). Through the activation of our Conscious and Subconscious Minds, we have the power to decide on how much energy to generate to put toward anything we want to accomplish. We activate our Conscious and Subconscious Minds through our visions, beliefs, attitudes, and value systems as they encounter our sensory perception mechanisms of what we see, smell, taste, hear, and touch. What we believe about what we see, smell, taste, hear, and touch is critical to how our mind engages to produce energy. In short, there is a direct correlation with what we see and believe about what we can do and the amount of energy generated to accomplish what we believe. So, like Ob-Wan Kenobi the master Jedi Master in "Star Wars" instructs Luke Skywalker that *"the force is with you,"* we say to all who read this book, ***"the force is within you."***

The *force within you* has a fixed capacity of energy production, and will generate only the right amount to accomplish work. Each person's energy capacity will be different depending on their physical health and their mental predisposition to utilize the **force within** to produce energy and to do work. Some people will have a greater capacity than others to generate high levels of energy, while others will have a smaller capacity and generate lower outputs of energy.

The size of your capacity to generate energy will be determined by your beliefs and attitudes transmitted through your Conscious Mind to your Subconscious Mind. Control over your beliefs and attitudes about the goals and objectives you desire to achieve and reach are connected to the amount of physical, mental, psychological, and spiritual energy that will be available to you to get the job done.

Key Insight

The energy generated by the **force within** is "pure energy," and should not be labeled as positive, negative, good or bad. It cannot be lost, destroyed or taken away; however, it can be mismanaged as in the case of working long periods of time without a break or rest. Thus, the key to the utilization of energy is balance between the amount of physical and mental energy generated to accomplish work.

Balance and the Utilization of Human Energy

Most people activate human energy from a "have to" perspective to live. The amount of physical energy generated is usually just enough to keep a person alive. Under these circumstances, a person can be expected to produce the minimal amount of work. Further, they will do just enough work to stay alive—creating an *"I have to do situation"* versus *"I choose to do situation."*

To produce mental energy one must hold the right attitudes and beliefs related to producing energy. The generation of physical and mental energies is interdependent and must be balanced to support an individual's ability to do work. This means that individuals must see the production of energy as an *"I want to versus I have to obligation."* Such a view of energy creates positive attitudes and beliefs that predispose an individual to whatever is necessary to create both physical and mental energy to accomplish the required work. The end result will be a balance between physical and mental energy.

The majority of humans use the major portion of their mental and physical energy to defend, to prevent, and for some **"have to"** purposes. Our core purpose in life is to stabilize and to survive. For growth we need to understand that energy should be applied towards **"want to"** purposes, deliberately moving through the point of balance. Imbalance between the utilization of mental and physical energy leads to an intense outflow of energy, fatigue, feelings of resentment, helplessness, and hopelessness.

In using Power Steps we want everyone to operate at the *"I want to"* level of utilizing physical and mental energy. An *"I want to"* attitude is the ideal and purest form of producing and utilizing energy, because it triggers the optimum use of mental and physical capacities.

As we leave the Principle of Energy, we hope each of you will take time out to examine both your physical and emotional energy levels. And if you find them in the least bit weak, you will make a commitment to strengthen them. We encourage you right now to commit to becoming stronger emotionally and physically. In fact, consider making great physical and emotional health a vision for yourself and apply the Power Step Principles to achieve them. Should you do that, then you will find the Principle of Self-Talk an invaluable key to realizing your vision.

SEVEN

SELF-TALK

Self-talk is the programmer of the Subconscious Mind
—Percy W. Thomas

What is Self-Talk?

Self-talk is the programmer of the Subconscious Mind. When we talk about self-talk in our workshops and show the Mind as a computer with the preponderance of the inputs being what we say to ourselves, participants get it. It is straight talk with yourself about what you must do to realize your vision, achieve results, establish relationships, be confident, sustain enthusiasm, and execute plans. So many of us rely solely on counselors, mentors, supervisors, preachers, teachers, and other people to talk to us about what we need to do to be successful in life. While all of these are good resources, we often ignore the most valuable resource for giving actionable advice—ourselves.

The notion that Self-talk is the programmer of the Subconscious Mind is also a frightening thought given how some people talk about others and themselves. Every word that you utter is heard by your Subconscious Mind. With its propensity to record everything you say in the first person all utterances refer to you. So, be very careful when you read something in this book that you disagree with and verbalize it as *"they don't know what they are talking about"* because your Subconscious Mind will interpret what you said as *"I don't know what I am talking about."* Your Self-talk impacts every aspect of your life whether you are aware of it or not.

Self-talk can affect how you see yourself in relationship to other people, as well as to how successful you are in reaching your Vision. In essence, your Self-talk impacts your self-image in a positive or negative way. Say negative things and you will have a negative self-image. Say positive things and it will produce a positive self-image. Yes, we are saying that your self-image is interdependent on how you talk about life events and interactions with others. Simply put, your self-talk projects your personality.

Some of us operate on the mistaken belief that because

they don't verbalize what they are thinking that they are not speaking. While your voice is a manifestation of your thoughts, for your Subconscious Mind to hear your thoughts they do not have to be expressed verbally. All you have to do is hold an internal dialogue with yourself and the Subconscious hears it and acts upon the information. It hears it clearly as if it is being broadcast through a loud speaker. Some of you have heard the old stories that if a person talks to himself that he must be crazy. Whenever, this subject comes up in our Power Steps workshops, Alice shares this story about my mother and me regarding Self-talk.

When Percy was a young boy, all his friends thought that a person who talked to themselves were crazy, and so it was disturbing for him to observe his mother talking to herself, which she did frequently. He was unaware that she was talking to herself to reinforce, motivate, and take action on something she needed to get done. He would hear her say things like *"Lillian you have to get yourself moving if you don't want to be late for work."* It appeared to him that his mother always needed to talk herself into doing what she needed to do. In hindsight, he recognizes that his mother had developed a technique for accomplishing what she needed to do, which is why we have incorporated Self-talk as one of the principles in this model that is needed to realize your desired goals/vision.

By talking to yourself you can boost your self-confidence, which you will need to be successful in any endeavor. Research has shown that people who engage in positive Self-talk about accomplishing their goals are more likely to achieve them than those who engage in negative Self-talk. Moreover, clinical researchers have found that individuals who engage in destructive Self-talk about themselves are more likely to become depressed and participate in harmful activities.

From a leadership perspective, researchers at the University of North Carolina have found that managers who showed strong leadership skills and creativity were those that engaged in constructive Self-talk. The research also revealed that managers who used negative Self-talk were more likely to be dysfunctional, avoid challenges placed in front of them, and focused on the negative aspects of challenging situations, rather than the positive aspects. Most often, managers that delved in negative Self-talk were also reluctant to initiate changes.

We want all readers to seriously consider the following aspects of Self-talk and to understand that it is a way to *release the force within* to do the following:

1. Build your confidence
2. Boost your self-esteem
3. Motivate yourself toward goal achievement.
4. Inspire yourself.

5. Encourage yourself to take action.
6. Apply the Power Steps Principles
7. Eliminate destructive behavior.
8. Eliminate irrational fears.
9. Focus on the positive.
10. Have more joy in your life.

Actionable Self-Talk

Actionable self-talk is self-counseling. Dr. Maxie Maultsby, Jr., the founder of Rational Behavior Therapy, states that the only counseling that works is self-counseling. He rationalizes that people generally respond to the advice they give themselves about what others tell them. Take for example two people who go to a counselor to stop smoking cigarettes. After six months, one person has stopped and the other continues to smoke. Both were counseled on healthy alternatives to smoking and the various support groups available to them during their withdrawal from smoking.

What attributes to one person stopping and the other person continuing to smoke is the quality of the self-talk. In the case of the person who stopped smoking, he or she counseled themselves to accept the advice of the counselor and to do exactly what they were advised to do. They said to themselves, *"The counselor has given me good advice and I am going to do everything they have told me."* In the case of the second person they said, *"The counselor is a worry wart and doesn't really know what they are talking about, and there is no real scientific evidence that smoking is bad."* Given the power of self-talk, it is not surprising to see the first person successfully stop smoking and the second person continuing to smoke until they are diagnosed with lung cancer. Thus, in applying the principle of Self-talk, we caution people to examine carefully what they think and say about the advice that is given to them.

Scripting Self-Talk

To be successful, you should script your Self-talk. We know scripting Self-talk is an unusual practice and one that you may not readily embrace. However, considering the harmful results related to the second person in the case sighted above regarding smoking, I would think that if scripting your Self-talk would help it is a small price to pay to possibly eliminate the devastating health impacts related to smoking.

What is scripting Self-talk? It is actually writing a script of what you are going to say to yourself regarding advice, events, situations, vision, goals, objectives, or work you are required to perform. It may also pertain to toxic or non-toxic relationships. The point here is not to leave your Self-talk to chance or events in situations in your life where you desire success. Self-talk must be purposeful, conscious, and consistent. By writing what you are going to say you ensure that the message that reaches your Subconscious Mind communicates exactly what you intended. After all, once your Self-talk is accepted on the Subconscious level of the Mind it will manifest in your behavior. You have no choice but to act upon the truth which is now stored in your subconscious. The power in scripting our Self-talk is that you can repeat verbally or silently with the same words and intention.

Writing Self-Talk Scripts

Self-talk scripts are written as simple statements concerning what you will or will not do regarding advice, counseling, events or situations you are likely to experience in life. The following is an example of a Self-talk script which applies to the smoking example above:

- "I must stop smoking or I will increase my risk of becoming ill and possibly die at an early age."
- "Today I have to stop smoking."
- "As of this moment, I no longer smoke cigarettes."

In the examples above, notice that the words that mean the most to your Subconscious are clear statements of your desire and intent.

Who Listens to Self-Talk

When you talk, **<u>you</u>** listen. The reason why we believe Self-talk is so powerful in getting people to take action is because when you talk to yourself you are your main audience. In applying the principle of Self-talk in your life, we want you to consciously use it to motivate yourself to achieve whatever you envision.

Self-Talk Triggers Action

If you want to ensure that you will accomplish anything you set for yourself, you must activate the principle of Self-talk. Self-talk triggers action(s) in you. When you use Self-talk to call yourself to action and it is received at the Subconscious level in your Mind, you are compelled to make it happen.

Talking to the Champ

Each of us has been endowed with our own personal champ inside of us: it is your Subconscious Mind or the *force within you*. Your Subconscious Mind represents the truth of everything you see, believe, feel, touch, taste, and smell. It is your central control center for generating your behavior related to achieving success. Therefore, we believe it is essential that whenever you decide to do something that is important to you, and it is not already programmed in the Subconscious, you should talk to the champ—the Subconscious Mind.

Life is full of changes that will take you on a roller coaster of emotional highs and lows. The road to success is full of opportunities for success and failures. When you run into low points on your success journey you need a way to instantly pick yourself up, Self-talk is that way. It will give you the inner strength to carry on and fight the good fight until victory is won. It will empower you to stand strong in the face of adversity and take on all challenges.

EIGHT

SPIRITUALITY

Spirituality is the essence of being in an enlightened state.
—Percy W. Thomas

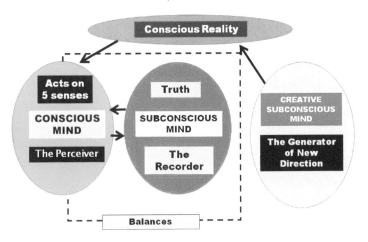

It has been difficult to write about Spirituality because the message we want to convey is not often spoken;

rather it is felt, expressed, and seen in our attitudes and behavior. Using our theory of the Mind, we believe that our Spirituality grows by our willingness to allow our Creative Subconscious to explore new ideologies, that are manifested in our Conscious Reality where it is seen and heard by others. Haven't you heard people refer to someone as having a "sweet spirit?" Clearly, they were saying that there is something about them. We believe Spirituality is the essence of who we are. Like a perfume our essence can be perceived as good or bad.

For example, how many times while watching a television program or a movie, have you been filled with emotions of joy and happiness, but you could not understand or explain the feelings. All you remember is that the characters in the movie evoked deep feelings of love and caring for others and it heightened your awareness of the need to personally extend yourself to be loving and caring toward people in need. How would you have labeled what you were feeling at the time? In Power Steps, we attribute those feelings as being spirit-filled. When good things happen in our lives that we can't explain, we tend to attribute them to Spirituality.

In the book, <u>Power Steps: 10 Principles of Success</u>, Percy stated he believed Spirituality is something akin to air. Air is everywhere and we need it to live and thrive, but it has no substantive form. One might say, air exists as "nothingness." However, this nothingness is required if we are to live and thrive.

The nothingness that Percy spoke of can be compared to the presence of the atom which is the building block of all matter. The atom exists with all its elements and components out of sight to the naked eye. Yet, it has the capacity to produce incredible energy and power. Thus, when we think of Spirituality, we think of an incredible energy source that produces power for human change and accomplishments. Because this power is unseen we believe that it must be activated. And, once activated and experienced it becomes Spirituality.

Our intent in this book is not to seek your agreement on what is Spirituality; rather, we would be quite content if this book caused you to reflect on how Spirituality has been a part of your life's story. The very acceptance that Spirituality has played a role in your life is acknowledgment that something greater than yourself exists in you. With agreement on the fact that Spirituality means different things to different folks, let's explore what Spirituality means in the context of this book.

With the atom as our frame of reference, we define Spirituality as being in an enlightened state of the force within to produce the energy and power to accomplish what you envision and believe you can obtain. To benefit from the power of the force within, you must believe and act without understanding. Some of you at this point are thinking where does this atom like power come from? This is a very good question.

Depending on your exposure in life to various philosophies, religions, and human beliefs you may designate different origins as the source of your Spirituality. Some may label the source as God, Creator, a higher power, or culture; while others may acknowledge they don't know. What you label your Spirituality is not as important as believing that it exists. To activate your power and put the force within to work for you, it must be connected to a strong belief. A belief so strong that it manifests itself in you as faith. Your faith is evidence that the source of your Spirituality (God, Higher Power, Culture, Philosophy) is in alignment.

We believe that by learning and applying all 10 principles you increase your ability to activate the principle of Spirituality in achieving your goals. Your Spirituality is a gift that must be nurtured and relied on to produce what you desire. As we develop the principle of Spirituality in this chapter, you will perhaps be left with the thought again that they do not know what they are talking about. Or perhaps this chapter will trigger in you a notion of Spirituality that is different from ours. If you should feel this way, then know that the spirit is working within you to come to an enlightened state. Also, know that Spirituality in the context of the **Power Steps** will mean different things to different people as we go on to share with you our thinking.

Recognizing Ones Spirituality

Recognizing ones Spirituality means you don't see with your eyes. Rather, you see through your connection with and the influence of your Creator/Higher Power[4] in your Subconscious Mind, which allows you to interpret what you see and experience.

The Creator/Higher Power in your life is responsible for the many gifts and talents you have; such as, your ability to love, care for others, think strategically, and succeed in life. Spirituality is responsible for your using the talents that the creator has given you to make a difference on the planet. Your gifts and talents are not intended to just serve your needs, but to make a difference in the lives of others. When you bring joy, happiness, peace, and comfort to others you are using your spiritual gifts and are effectively applying the principle of Spirituality. To apply the principle of Spirituality you must send to your **Conscious Mind** via your **Conscious Reality** positive or negative actions or thoughts. When these thoughts are received

---

4   We intentionally use the terminology "Creator and Higher Power" out of respect for different beliefs, religions, and cultures.

and reside in the **Subconscious Mind** as truths they become the basis of your Spirituality.

In the context of the principle of Spirituality, you must understand that you are both spiritual and human. When we understand that we are spiritual and human, we can then accept our relationship to our higher power. Ultimately, Spirituality may be simply expressed as the demonstration of our revealed faith.

Spirituality is based in love and good deeds. The principles Vision, Belief, Competence, Concentration, Confidence, Enthusiasm, Energy, Self-talk, and Action are dependent on Spirituality and must be based in love to achieve maximum effectiveness. True Spirituality may manifest the positive characteristics of love, kindness, trust, faith, peace, and a sense of well-being in all that you strive to achieve.

Spirituality and Action

Spirituality allows us to circumvent our ego and to embrace opportunities that present themselves through the force within. Spirituality also enables each of us to see beyond our limitations and perspectives to see the "big picture" and move toward that which we envision.

Spirituality strengthens your resolve to take action while knowing that it is the will of the Creator/Higher

Power, and therefore what is being done is for more than **personal gratification and benefit**. Thus, Spirituality is a prerequisite for the final principle of A*ction,* which will be covered in the next and final chapter.

NINE

ACTION

In the first book the principle of Action was simply stated as applying the 10 Principles in your personal and professional life. We have come to realize that Action is much more than just applying the principles. Taking action is the most important step you can take in keeping your Vision alive. Taking no action yields no result, and all your work and learning will have been just another academic exercise. Simply put no action no gain. Thus, the actions you take after reading this book will make all the difference in the world as to whether you achieve the success you desire. If you guessed we are saying the Action principle is about planning, you are right on point. Yes, you must create a written Action Plan to follow, however, the principle of Action is much more than simply writing a plan. In Power Steps, Action includes more than just capturing your vision, goals and objectives on paper. Millions of individuals across the world have done that with very little success to show for their efforts. Therefore, we strongly suggest that before you finalize your plan you consider the following:

(1) Examine Your Vision

We suggest that to enhance your chance of success your Vision should have a meaningful purpose. Does it allow you to stretch and ask yourself what are the broader implications for you and others?

(2) Know What You Need To Know

There will always be things that you need to know and have control of in accomplishing your Vision. Think about your Vision and identify the competencies you need to have or learn to realize your Vision. Determine if you need them or if you can hire someone with them to do what you want. If it is something that you must have set a date and time frame for when you will have them.

(3) Who do you need to know?

You might think it is a cliché that success is result of

who you know. In Power Steps, we believe that networking with the right people is one way of building the right connections. So, reach out and get to know the people that can help you succeed.

(4) Being in the Right Place at the Right Time

Every day across the world and in your neighborhood opportunities related to your Vision and goals are happening. You don't know about them because you are not present. You have to be present to take advantage of opportunities. Thus, it is important for you to stay abreast of things that are happening related to what you want to do and where possible attend them. Affiliate with as many groups and organizations that align with and support your Vision as possible. Another key to success is being in the right place at the right time.

(5) Create Your Inner Circle

Despite what you may have heard about picking yourself up by your boot straps on your own, we believe success is always a collective process. Think through and select three confidantes whom you trust to make up your inner circle of friends. Use them to bounce your ideas and plans off of before making final decisions.

(6) Create Your Go to Team

Select a team of approximately nine people with vary-ing degrees of expertise and contacts who you trust and who share your values regarding your Vision and projects. Because you will need to rely on them to get things done, they must be credible people.

(7) Social Media Outreach

Develop your social media contacts so that you will have an easy way of communicating with people about your Vision and projects. Once you established your social media contacts stay in touch.

(8) Brand Yourself

Develop your personal brand so that others will know who you are and what you stand for. It allows people to know what you are passionate about and what things they can expect from you. Your brand affects other people's decisions about your intelligence, character, and ability. It will determine if they want to associate with you or align with your Vision.

(9) Create an Elevator Speech

An elevator speech is a short speech or pitch

(approximately 30 seconds) that is designed to get a conversation started about your Vision or project. Since it is likely to be a chance encounter, your speech should not get into every detail of your Vision or project. All you want to do is make sure the person you are talking to understands what you are talking about and is interested enough to find out more about it. Your goal is to get an appointment in which you can share more information.

(10) Pray

Pray to your higher power for clarity and success regarding your Vision or project. In your prayers be sure to ask for what you want. Make your prayers specific and detailed about the actions needed to obtain your desired outcome.

Webster's New World Dictionary defines action as "the doing of something; state of being in motion or working." In Power Steps, action is defined as intentional behavior ensuing from the application of the principles of Vision, Belief, Competence, Concentration, Confidence, Enthusiasm, Energy, Self-talk, and Spirituality to produce a desired result. Doing it is easier said than done. Therefore, implicit in the principle of Action is the concept of planning.

At a lecture to a group of master's level students, in

the renowned Johns Hopkins University's Leadership Development Program, we heard the statement, "leaders must plan to: <u>know</u>, <u>be</u>, <u>plan</u>, and <u>do</u>." Of all the profound things we heard in the lecture, the words "know, be, plan and do" resonated and caused us to think about the principle of Action in our book. As we thought about these four powerful words, we formed the acronym KBPD. KBPD is the trigger for activating the 10 Principles and makes them relevant in accomplishing the goals you set. What follows is a brief description of each word that makes up the KBPD acronym.

Know

The concept of Know means you must know your Vision (seeing in your mind's eye the Vision) and seeing yourself realizing the Vision. Know also refers to the knowledge needed to successfully realize your Vision. Vision and knowledge interacting together creates a map or a global positioning system (GPS), which allows you to make real your Vision.

Many of us will not hesitate to use a map or GPS to guide us in reaching a destination, especially when it comes to traveling somewhere for the first time. The same principle applies to reaching one's Vision because it is a picture of a place you have never been. Without a map of the territory showing the path to your destination, any road will get you there. And, when you take any road, most often you will arrive somewhere that you don't want to be. Knowing all aspects of where you want to go in advance ensures that you will know when you have reached the correct destination.

Having a map of the territory and seeing your destination in your mind is not enough, you must see yourself getting to where you want to go. On the road to success, you may encounter many obstacles and impediments placed in your path. It is important that you not let those barriers derail you and take you off course or keep you from getting to your destination—making real your Vision. After you know where you want to go, you have to "Be."

Be

In this book, **Be** implies action beyond existing or survival. **Be** means to take on the necessary characteristics and persona to achieve your goals and the mechanism that unlocks your Creative Subconscious. **Be** is acting in many different roles to apply the multiple skill sets necessary to ensure that you reach your vision. Moreover, **Be** means that you must be fully present in relation to the project or task you commit to undertake. In being fully present, you must prepare yourself to learn and apply many different skill sets necessary to reach your goals and objectives. It is worth stating again that it is absolutely critical that you learn to be fully present in any endeavor and quickly acquire the necessary skills to be successful.

In many ways, **Be** means you have to develop the skill of an actor, which allows an individual to enter in and out of the roles they need to play. Yes, acting lessons will help you develop the comfort with different roles and skills that are required to be successful. Acting out the **Be** roles in your life allows you to prepare for being successful without the risk of failure.

According to Margaret Mead, role-playing is an excellent way to learn because a portion of every role an individual plays becomes truth in the Subconscious Mind. We have already established that the Subconscious Mind is the regulator of our human software: our attitudes, values, beliefs and behavior. Thus, learning which stems from role-playing is received and stored on the Subconscious level and will cause a person to automatically **Be**. In this sense, to **Be** becomes habitual and will support the investment of your time, energy, and personal commitment to produce a successful outcome.

Plan

Webster's New World Dictionary defines **Plan** as a scheme or program for making, doing, or arranging something; a project, design, schedule, etc. In this book, the 10 Principles are a road map that lays out specific steps to be followed to achieve success in realizing your vision, goals and objectives. Though the principles are written and available to all who purchase this book, they have no power or meaning until you decide to personalize them and own them.

Owning the 10 Principles—Power Steps Plan

To own the 10 Principles, we recommend that you develop a one-page plan for each principle using the outline below. Make your Plan realistic by establishing achievable dates and deadlines. Once your Plan is written, you must follow it each day until it becomes a habit. Any Plan that you follow for at least 21 consecutive days will become a habit.

Vision:

Write a clear vision statement that incorporates what has been taught in this book.

Belief:

Write three positive beliefs about your vision.

Competence:

List three things you must become competent in to support the realization of your vision.

Concentration:

Meditate each day on your vision, beliefs about your vision, and the three things you must master to support your vision.

Confidence:

Identify three things you will do each day to reinforce your confidence with respect to realizing your vision.

Enthusiasm:

List three things you will do each day to show enthusiasm for your vision.

Energy:

Develop a nutritional eating plan for the week and exercise 15 minutes in the morning and 15 minutes in the evening.

Self-talk:

Write a short positive affirmation statement regarding your having accomplished your dream.

<u>Spirituality</u>:

Spend 10 minutes meditating in the morning after tak-ing a shower, and 10 minutes at night before going to bed.

<u>Action</u>:

The guidelines above provide you with action steps that you can take every day, but we believe that to stay on track you should establish a support group to hold you accountable and provide encouragement. We have seen the effectiveness of this approach in groups like Weight Watchers, Alcoholics Anonymous, and cohort learners. There is no doubt that it works, especially when one has a planned approach to follow.

Putting your Plan in writing and working your Plan daily brings all 10 principles in play and creates the de-sired success in your life. These simple principles have worked for us and will work for you. You have taken the first step by reading this book; the second step is to write your one-page Power Steps Plan. This plan will evoke the KBPD acronym in your Conscious and Subconscious Mind, placing you on automatic pilot to make real your Vision.

PROLOGUE

POWER STEPS: RELEASING THE FORCE WITHIN

In this book you have the secrets to realize your dreams and hopes for the future. You must first read it at least six times, or until you have fully absorbed all 10 principles into your Subconscious Mind. You then must commit to applying the principles as part of your daily life activities. After you start practicing the principles, you will begin to see and experience changes in your life. And, the more you use the principles the more proficient you will become in attracting to you everything needed to accomplish your goals. The process of applying the principles becomes less complicated as you use them.

When you experience success using the principles, you

will feel empowered to take on any challenge or opportunity. You will come to appreciate the f**orce within you** that makes it possible for you to have success doing incredible things. You can take comfort in knowing that Power Steps based on the science of repetition works, and by repeating positive beliefs and behaviors you will have a contagious impact on other people who will see your success and wish to emulate it.

Once you read Power Steps and decide to use the principles you will be on your way to *releasing the force within you* to create success for you and others. Each principle builds on each other to release the force. Each time that you use the force within you are able to access the power quicker.

One caution we want to leave you with is that Power Steps works for destructive purposes as well as good ones. We encourage you to use these amazing principles to enrich your life and the lives of those you encounter. So, *"go forth and release the force within you!"*

ABOUT THE AUTHORS

PERCY W. THOMAS, SC.D.

Percy W. Thomas received his Bachelor of Science degree from Maryland State College (currently known as the University of Maryland Eastern Shore), a Masters of Education from Coppin State College, which is now Coppin State University, and the Doctorate of Science degree from Johns Hopkins University. He also holds certificates in leadership from Harvard University, The League for Innovation and the Federal Executive Institute. Dr. Thomas is a retired Captain from the United States Public Health Service, and retired again as a civilian from the U.S. Senior Executive Service.

As a researcher, Dr. Thomas has conducted qualitative

research on inner-city juvenile gangs. Published numerous papers and served on several dissertation committees. He is a former Professor in the internationally recognized Johns Hopkins University Leadership Development Institute, the Morgan State University Community College Doctoral Leadership program, and he serves on the USDA Graduate School Leadership Advisory Board.

Dr. Thomas has developed and implemented several national training programs on leadership, success, motivation, achieving excellence, multicultural workforce practices, management principles, basic supervisory practices, and he has conducted numerous program evaluations and organizational climate assessments in the public and private sectors.

Dr. Thomas is noted for his work with Lewis Brown Griggs, President of Griggs Productions, in his award winning seven-part video series Valuing Diversity. He is the author and inventor of the <u>Cultural Rapport Model: Fostering Harmony in the Workplace</u>, <u>Take Charge of Your Career Institute</u>, and author of <u>Power Steps: Ten Principles of Success</u>. In June 2016, Dr. Thomas co-authored a new book titled, <u>Playing the Career Game</u>.

ALICE H. THOMAS, PH.D.

Dr. Thomas is the President of MyCareerTarget, LLC (MCT), which is a consulting firm located in Maryland, and Chief Mentor for Success Business Inc (SBI). Both companies specialize in leadership training and development, and organizational climate assessments.

She earned a Doctor of Philosophy in Educational Leadership from the Union Institute and University, a Master of Science in Applied Behavioral Science and Organizational Development from Johns Hopkins University, and a Bachelor of Science degree in Program Administration from Antioch University.

Dr. Thomas' career includes significant experiences in federal government, academia, and the private sector. In 1996, she retired from the federal government as Chief of Grants and Contracts for the Bureau of Primary Health Care, Health Resources and Services Administration, U.S. Department of Health and Human Services. She also served at the National Institutes of Health, Peace Corps, and Smithsonian Institute. As Chief of Grants and Contracts, she managed grant budgets in excess of two billion dollars for the National Institute of Child Health and Human, National Institute of Human Genome, and the Bureau of Primary Health Care. For her creativity and ingenuity in grants management, Dr. Thomas received the Distinguished Service award from the Secretary of the Department of Health and Human Services.

She has designed and led several major organizational change processes, conducted numerous organizational climate assessments, and coached several executives. She is certified as a Career Development Counselor and in 2011 developed a course titled, <u>Effective Career Development Management</u>, which she has taught to hundreds of government employees.

In academia, Dr. Thomas has been an instructor, administrator, and principal investigator. As an administrator and researcher at Sojourner-Douglass College, Dr. Thomas served as Executive Assistant to the President, Co-Director of the College's School of Graduate Studies, Director of Sponsored Programs and Applied Research, and Principal Investigator on several grants in the field of Health Disparities. Additionally, Dr. Thomas has served as adjunct faculty for Johns Hopkins University and Sojourner-Douglass College.

BIBLIOGRAPHY

Abdul-Karim, Zayd. <u>7 Steps in Deep Transitions</u>: <u>A Spiritual Guide to Peace of Mind, Prosperity, and Success</u>. Springfield, Virginia: development training systems, 2005

Blanchard, Ken. <u>The Heart of a Leader</u>. Colorado Springs, Colorado: Honor Books, 1999

Boldt, Lawrence G. <u>How To Be, Do, or Have Anything</u>. Berkeley, California: Ten Speed Press, 2001

Canfield, Jack, Hansen, Mark V. and Hewitt, Les. <u>The Power of Focus</u>. Deerfield Beach, Florida: Health Communications, Inc., 2000

Carlson, Richard. <u>Don't Sweat The Small Stuff: And It's All Small Stuff</u>. New York: Hyperion, 1997

Clement, Pierre. <u>Power Hypnosis: A Guide for Faster Learning and Greater Self-Mastery</u>. Glendale, California: Westwood Publishing Company, 1979

Chopra, Deepak. <u>The Seven Spiritual Laws of Success</u>. San Raphael, California: New York World Library, 1994

Coats, Steve, Heuer, Tom. <u>There Is No Box</u>. Provo, Utah: Executive Excellence Publishing, 2007

Ellis, Albert. <u>New Guide To Rational Living</u>. Hollywood, California: Wilshire Book Company, 1975

Ellis, Albert. <u>Reason and Emotion In Psychotherapy</u>. New York: Lyle Stuart, 1963

Frankl, Viktor. <u>Silent Spring</u>. Boston, Massachusetts: Beacon Press, 1992

Griggs, Lewis B, and Louw, Lente-Louise. <u>Valuing Diversity: New Tools for A New Reality</u>. New York, McGraw Hill, Inc., 1994

Hines, Joseph E. <u>A Personal Walk</u>. Elkridge, Maryland: SBI Publishing, 2008

Johnson, Bill. <u>The Supernatural Power of a Transformed Mind</u>. Shippensburg, PA: Destiny Image Publishers, Inc., 2005